ASTON VILLA

Double Winners 1896/97

A 'WINNING SEASON' SERIES

•

Copyright © Sports Projects Ltd, 1996

•

Compiled and published in England by
SPORTS PROJECTS LTD
188 Lightwoods Hill, Smethwick, Warley, West Midlands B67 5EH

•

ISBN 0 946866 36 8

•

Printed in England

INTRODUCTION

● The idea for this publication came from a suggestion by Rod Evans – an avid researcher of the Club's history – that the centenary of Aston Villa's 'double' success in season 1896/97 should be commemorated in some way.

The achievement is unique in Villa's 122-year history; only the League Championship win in 1981, coupled with the European Cup triumph a season later, measures comparison.

So difficult is the League and Cup 'double' to accomplish that just six clubs have completed the feat in English football history; Preston North End (1889), Aston Villa (1897), Tottenham Hotspur (1961), Arsenal (1971), Liverpool (1986), and Manchester United (1994 and 1996).

The story of Villa's 'double' is presented here as it unfolded in season 1896/97 using reports and comments taken from publications of the day.

There are reports for all first team fixtures, as well as friendly and minor cup matches, plus week-to-week comment on club affairs. Also included is a selection of advertisements that appeared in the local journals at the time of Queen Victoria's Golden Jubilee.

Very few Villa photographs survive from that era; therefore our picture content is somewhat limited and has been supplemented with illustrations used by some of the newspapers of the time.

The 'double' season was also the period when the Club moved home from Wellington Road, Perry Barr, to the Aston Lower Grounds and a new stadium that became known as Villa Park. By then the 'double' had already been won and proved a fitting memorial for the old ground that the 'Perry Pets' had occupied for more than 20 years.

Seventeen players were used in all League and English Cup games. They were: James Whitehouse, Howard Spencer, Albert Evans, Jack Reynolds, James and John Cowan, James Crabtree, Charlie Athersmith, John Devey, Johnny Campbell, Fred Wheldon, Tommy Wilkes, James Welford, Jeremiah Griffiths, Fred Burton, Bob Chatt and Steve Smith.

Some were 'stars' – others shone a little less brightly. But whatever status they held, their contribution to the 'double' achievement has ensured that none of their names will ever be forgotten in Aston Villa's glorious history.

Bernard Gallagher
Editor
October 1996

BIBLIOGRAPHY

The Birmingham Daily Gazette
The Birmingham Daily Post
The Birmingham Daily Mail
The Sports Argus
The Owl
The Birmingham Pictorial & Dart
The Grasshopper

◊

PHOTOGRAPHY

Aston Villa FC plc
Colorsport Ltd
Draycott
Powls & May
Sports Projects Ltd
Tippetts
Albert Wilkes

◊

DESIGN & LAYOUT

Bernard Gallagher

◊

TYPESETTING

Vic Millward

◊

PROOF READING

Vic Millward
Rod Evans

◊

PRINTING

Polar Print & Publishing Ltd

◊

SPECIAL THANKS

Local Studies Department of the
Birmingham Central Library
Rod Evans
Aston Villa Football Club
Derrick Spinks
Jon Farrelley

◊

DEDICATION

This book is dedicated to the memory of
the Aston Villa men who achieved the
double success of winning
the Football League and English Cup
in season 1896/97.

THE FOOTBALL CAMPAIGN: A FEW NOTES

● Once again the flight of time has brought us within a few hours of the football season; the newspapers are crowded with county averages – the sure forerunner of the end of the summer's cricket – and almost by the time these notes appear next week the whirr of the ball and the swish of the bat will have been heard for the last time in this year of grace.

It is needless to say how eagerly the football season – especially during the last fortnight – has been anticipated by thousands of devotees who week by week follow the fortune of their particular clubs. The parrot cry that was raised when professionalism was first legalised that the death-knell of the winter game had been sounded has long since been consigned to oblivion, and if we may judge from the experience of recent years there is every indication that its popularity increases by leaps and bounds as each season comes around. In point of numbers present, in gate receipts, and in keenness of competition the football of 1895-6 exceeded all previous records, but I believe the season that is just breaking upon us will go one better.

The revision of rules which takes place annually in June produced nothing of a startling character. The attempts to limit the within which a penalty kick could be given failed, but a move in the right direction has been made in leaving it to the referee to decide whether an offence which has been committed within the penalty line is intentional or not. Under the old rule a referee had no option but to allow a penalty kick on appeal in the event of a trip or a 'foul' play, but I am clearly of opinion that the wielder of the whistle should have a discretionary power in the event of the offence not being wilful. Moreover, the referee can now award a penalty kick without appeal, and this, too, I think, is an excellent move, for I am a firm believer in the referee in having almost unlimited powers.

It can, I think, be taken for granted that in League Football, at all events, the officials who are appointed are competent men, and now that they are to be assisted in their important labours by the services of neutral linesmen every facility should be given them, and every reasonable power placed in their hands, so that football may be brought to the highest stage of perfection. The appointment of neutral linesmen is one of the best moves the League has made, for not only will there be less club-feeling shown, but the referee will have the valuable aid of independent officials whom he can consult with perfect confidence on any debatable point.

It is with the knowledge of this great improvement in the government of the game that I most sincerely regret that the rule relating to free kicks is not to be altered this season, after all. The Football Association approved of the proposal to give referees 'discretion' in regards to 'hands,' thereby enabling them to award free kicks or not, according to whether it was their opinion that the handling was intentional or not. Everyone knows what an enormous waste of time and vexation arise in the course of a game from free kicks, which have to be given for the purely accidental handling of the ball, and everyone would have welcomed a change in the laws which would have avoided all this. The Football Association, as I have said, approved of the alteration which would have avoided this waste of time, but unfortunately the proposal was not submitted to the International Board in time, and, though the latter body discussed it, the resolution could not be dealt with officially. In this respect, therefore, the laws remain in 'status quo,' and we shall have to wait another year before this much-needed improvement can be made.

Beyond the points to which I have draw attention, there are no alterations of any importance and the game will be played under pretty much the same conditions as heretofore.

THE OBSERVER

● Aston Villa, as champions of the League, claim first attention, and it is pretty safe to assume that the devoted followers of the Perry Barr brigade are on very good terms with themselves. 'On paper' there should be nothing to beat the Villa; but paper form is very often deceptive, and it will be well for everyone to wait to see how the men shape on the field when they have earnest and determined opponents against them before 'counting their chickens.' Still, there need be no hesitation in saying that the Villa start with every prospect of a successful career.

They have retained the services of the whole of the players who helped them to so many memorable victories last year, and they have strengthened one or two weak places by the engagement of Wheldon, of Small Heath; Whitehouse of Grimsby Town; George of Trowbridge and Bristol; Private Harris of the Coldstream Guards; and one or two promising local players.

A good deal has been written and said about the prohibitive prices paid by the Villa for Wheldon and Whitehouse; but after all I don't think there will be much to grumble at if the men prove their worth, as there is every reason to hope. Wheldon has long been the shining light of Small Heath, and on his best form he should prove to be a source of strength to the Villa vanguard, though it remains to be seen whether the proposal to put him on the right wing with Athersmith will work as satisfactorily as though he were kept in his usual position at inside left. In the last two practice matches he has certainly given indication of proving a useful partner to the fleet-footed right winger, and if the scheme works out right the Villa ought to have a fine vanguard with Athersmith, Wheldon, Devey, Campbell and John Cowan – to say nothing of such useful candidates as Smith and Chatt, with Crabtree as emergency man.

There will be the old half-back line – Reynolds, James Cowan and Crabtree – a trio that will be difficult to beat when at their best. Last year Reynolds was not so successful as he had been, but from personal observation, I can say I never saw him looking better, and I shall be greatly surprised if he does not retain his position. As reserves in this department the Villa have such useful players as Chatt, Fred Burton and Griffiths – the last-named a very promising youngster, who distinguished himself with the second team.

Welford and Spencer, who bore the brunt of defence last year with such conspicuous success, will form the mainstay of the 'last line,' both men appearing to be in capital trim. Welford's season with Warwickshire has evidently done him a lot of good, for he has considerably improved his pace.

The goalkeeping will rest between last year's custodian, Wilkes, and the Grimsby acquisition, Whitehouse, with George – a finely-built young fellow over six feet high – as reserve.

Evans and Bourne (of Kidderminster) are a couple of promising young backs, with plenty of pluck and dash, and should develop into capable men, whilst much is expected of Private E. J. Harris of the Coldstream Guards, who has shown considerable skill as a centre forward. It is expected that he will be at the service of the Villa in about three weeks, he and George having already been signed on League forms.

Several other youngsters from neighbouring clubs have been tried during the practice matches, but without disclosing anything of exceptional merit.

It remains only to be said that the Villa will continue to play at Perry Barr for some months to come, for the new ground at Aston cannot be got ready until the spring. They play their opening match against Small Heath tomorrow evening at the Wellington Road enclosure, and meet Stoke in a League game the following evening at the same ground. On Saturday they play their old rivals the Albion at Stoney Lane.

LOWER GROUNDS DELAY

● Aston Villa as League Champions of last season, are certainly deserving of mention, for they are undoubtedly the most popular club in the district, while no team draws larger attendances away from home than they. The Villa's new home at the Aston Lower Grounds is not yet completed, and although the work is rapidly being gone on with, there is no prospect of it being ready this side of Christmas. Indeed it is scarcely probable that the ground will be used at all until the season 1897-8, though there is some talk of inviting a big Scotch club – such as Celtic or Queen's Park – down to celebrate the opening of the new ground towards the close of the forthcoming season.

VILLA GO FROM STRENGTH TO STRENGTH

● The Villa team should, if anything, be slightly stronger than was the case last season, for, with the exception of Dennis Hodgetts (who has at last decided to retire from active service), the whole of last year's first team players have been re-engaged, while the committee have also secured two first-class men in Whitehouse, the brilliant goalkeeper from Grimsby Town, and Freddy Wheldon, the Small Heath left-wing forward. Another player who has been booked is Bourne, a full back from Kidderminster, who has already made himself popular here by reason of his clever play in the practice games. The position which has not been satisfactorily strengthened is that of right-back; Reynolds was in very poor form last season, and unless he has recovered his old ability the committee may find themselves in a quandary. Burton is not class enough to play regularly, and it is probable that Chatt may be re-introduced into the first eleven.

SMITH ON STANDBY

● No club in the kingdom possesses a finer quintette of forwards than the Villa. Athersmith and Devey make a magnificent right-wing pair, Campbell is a good centre, and Wheldon and John Cowan on the left will want a lot of beating. Everyone is pleased that Steve Smith has recovered from the injury which kept him off the football field the greater part of last season, and will be ready to resume when required. Until one of the other five gets injured or goes off form, it is scarcely likely that Smith will regain his old position. Of course it is unfortunate for him, but John Cowan was treated similarly last season, so he will have no cause for grumbling.

WHY NOT WELFORD?

● In previous years, when Warwickshire have required Jack Devey's services in the cricket field, the Aston Villa committee have let him off training. Yet Welford has been refused permission to play in Warwickshire's two last games v Leicestershire and Derbyshire. Why this distinction?

SAILOR DUNNING

● Many folks are doubtless ignorant as to what has become of William Dunning, who was connected with Aston Villa for several seasons. After his engagement with the Villa terminated (in 1895) he disappeared from the football world, and it was not until I met him at Southampton a fortnight ago that I learned how he was going on. He is employed on a boat sailing between England and America, and the work appears to agree with him, for he looks far healthier than he did when in Birmingham.

BRIEFLETS...

☞ *BAIRD, the old Villa back, is playing for the Clyde (Glasgow).*

☞ *INGLIS, the new Small Heath forward, comes with 'a good reputation.' Did any player ever come with a bad one?*

Thursday 27th August 1896
PROBABLES 3, IMPROBABLES 1

● A practice match was played last evening at Perry Barr between two elevens of the above club, before a large and appreciative crowd. Capital form was shown, but, as might be gathered from the names of the sides, the Probables proved successful, the score being 3 goals to 1 in their favour. The teams were:

Probables: Wilkes, goal; Spencer and Welford, backs; Reynolds, James Cowan, Crabtree, half-backs; Athersmith, Wheldon, Devey, Campbell and John Cowan, forwards. Improbables: Whitehouse, goal; Evans and Bourne, Backs; Griffiths, Chatt and Burton, half-backs; Woolfull, Flannagan, Rideout, Harvey and Smith, forwards.

A committee meeting was held subsequently, at which the following teams were selected for the opening matches at Perry Barr next Tuesday against Small Heath (friendly) and on Wednesday against Stoke (League).

Against Small Heath: George or Whitehouse, goal; Spencer and Welford, backs; Burton, James Cowan and Crabtree, half-backs; Athersmith, Wheldon, Devey, Campbell and Smith, forwards.

Against Stoke: Wilkes, goal; Spencer and Welford, backs; Reynolds, James Cowan and Crabtree, half-backs; Athersmith, Wheldon, Devey, Campbell and John Cowan, forwards.

George was last year goalkeeper for the Bristol Association in the match against the Villa, when he gave an exceptionally good display. He has already been signed as a League player for the Villa.

Tuesday 1st September 1896
VILLA 3, SMALL HEATH 1

● There were about 3,000 people present at Perry Barr to witness the opening match of the season. The weather was fine, but decidedly autumn-like.

Play opened quietly, the Villa defending the entrance goal. Twice the home left-wing got away, and Smith sent the ball wide on each side of the goal with successive shots. Edwards then got down into the Villa half, only to be checked by Spencer, and returning to the attack the Villa drew first blood, Wheldon scoring with a shot that hit the inside of the goal post and glanced into the opposite corner of the net. The same player was not too long in scoring a second point, the Villa forwards at the time crowding the visiting goal.

Again Edwards got loose down the left, but his centre was turned to poor account. Later on Robertson and Inglis put in a pretty bit of work on the right, a really good shot from the first-named being well saved by the Villa keeper. Wheldon passed prettily to his partner on the outside, and Devey got a chance of heading into goal, but Pointer smartly fisted away. A capital rush by Small Heath very nearly ended in the capture of the Villa goal, the ball hitting the post and rebounding into play. Athersmith was then given an opening by Cowan, but nothing came of it, and Edwards was pulled up for offside after a fine chance had been thrown away in front of the visitor's goal. When Small Heath got a free kick in front of the home goal owing to a foul by Crabtree they had a chance, but the ball was worked away, and just on the verge of half-time the Villa only just failed to add another point. At the interval the score was Villa 2, Small Heath 0.

The home forwards were quickly away on restarting, first Crabtree and then Devey missed by inches only. The first corner fell to the Villa but nothing came of it. A couple of corner kicks followed to the visitors, and then Athersmith did a fine sprint and shot closely over the bar. From a free kick in a good position there were a few quick passes in front of the Villa posts, and

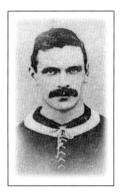

JACK DEVEY'S BENEFIT

● Derby County are coming to Perry Barr on Monday, October 5th, to play a friendly game with Villa for Jack Devey's benefit. Dot the date down in your diary, please, for if ever a football player deserved a good benefit, the Villa skipper does.

FRIENDLY DAYS ARE FINISHED

● Eager as many football enthusiasts have been for the opening of the season, the meagre attendance at the Villa ground on Tuesday evening added fresh proof that the days of 'friendly' matches are over, both from a financial and spectacular point of view. It will be understood, of course, that by friendly matches is meant those games played outside any of the numerous competitions. All told, there would not be many more than 3,000 spectators present to welcome the players, and of this number it may be safely said that the large majority went away anything but gratified with the entertainment provided. On the Villa side Smith made his reappearance in the first team, but was palpably out of condition. The players in the front divisions did not appear to find their feet very smartly, the bulk of the effective work being done by the halves and backs. Bearing in mind the fact that the Small Heath team had been entirely re-organised, and that their best forward in the person of Wheldon was opposed to them, it was not unnaturally anticipated that the Villa would have little difficulty in polishing off the visitors with ease. This is just what they did not do.

THE HEATHEN!

● It seemed like the irony of fate that Fred Wheldon should be the player to open the scoring account against his old club this season. 'Twas too cruel!

MATCH OF THE SEASON

● 'The match of the season,' as some folks always speak of League games between the Villa and the Albion, takes place at West Bromwich tomorrow, and there should be a record attendance for the Stoney Lane ground. No matter how these two clubs may fare in other games, there is always a keen struggle for supremacy when they meet, and 'paper form' is never of any account whatever. Of course the Villa ought to win right enough, and they probably will do so, but if the margin is a large one it will be a big surprise to everyone.

BRIEFLETS...

↪ *David Skea, the erstwhile Aston Villa forward, who for the past two seasons has been with Leicester Fosse, has joined Swindon Town, and is partnering Hallam (late of Small Heath) on the right wing.*

↪ *The Small Heath ground has been greatly improved during the close season; the same cannot be said of the team.*

↪ *Billy Dickson, the old Villa player, takes a benefit at Stoke shortly, and is anxious to secure the services of the Villa.*

↪ *The cricket match between eleven Muffs and Duffs and an eleven selected from the Aston Villa Football Club (past and present) will be played on Wednesday next at the County Ground. It is to be hoped that fine weather will favour the venture, for the proceeds are to be given to the Birmingham hospitals, and there has already been one postponement. A good day's sport should result.*

the visitors put on their first goal. Directly afterwards the Villa crowded the Small Heath goal, but although many attempts were made no score resulted, Athersmith putting the ball over the corner of the goal. Play was not exciting after this, the spectators getting few chances to cheer, although there was a bout of laughter when Welford was bowled head over heels. A good run by Smith resulted in a corner, and from the flag-kick Crabtree neatly scored, the goalkeeper failing to keep out a curly one. With darkness creeping on the game lost much of its interest, and with nearly a quarter of an hour to play the referee stopped the game, the ball being followed at the time with great difficulty. A somewhat tame game ended: Villa 3, Small Heath 1.

Aston Villa: Whitehouse; Welford and Spencer; Crabtree, Cowan and Burton; Smith, Campbell, Devey, Wheldon and Athersmith.

Small Heath: Pointer; Dunlop and Lester; Farnall, Leake and Walton; Inglis, Robertson, Jones, Abbott and Edwards.

LEAGUE DIVISION ONE

Wednesday 2nd September 1896
VILLA 2, STOKE 1

● The more serious work of the Villa season was opened last evening at Perry Barr when Stoke opposed them in the first League match. Dull but fine weather prevailed, the engagement attracting fully 6,000 spectators.

Kicking up the hill at the commencement, and against the slight wind, the Villa were first aggressive, but Eccles defended sturdily, and for some moments the game swung backwards and forwards pretty evenly. Welford and Spencer were a bit uncertain for a moment or two, but quickly steadied themselves, and the home front string getting away well together, Campbell gave John Cowan a pretty pass, and running on the latter put the finish on a nice piece of work by scoring a fine goal, the ball glancing through off the goalkeeper's hands. Fouls were frequent, both sides being penalised, and from a free kick to Stoke the Villa goal was threatened for a time, Wilkes however, being quite equal to the task imposed on him. There was a slight delay owing to one of the visiting forwards being slightly hurt in a charge, and after the ball had been tossed up the Villa ran in a good style to the opposite end. Campbell worked in a nice opening and sent in a rattling shot, which Latham hit out feebly, and Devey had no difficulty in scoring a second goal. Midfield work was uninteresting, but Stoke had a turn at the Villa end, where they found the Villa defence sound. Both Devey and Cowan had splendid openings but shot weakly. Dickson, at half, gave the Stoke right a few fair chances, and after Simpson had been loudly cheered for a grand long shot into Wilkes's hands, Maxwell just shaved the post on the wrong side. The Villa continued to have rather the best of play up to half-time, the score then reading: Villa 2, Stoke 0.

Play was carried on at the visitor's end when the game was continued, and after Stoke had enjoyed a quick run into Villa quarters Athersmith returned. Good work by Campbell was spoilt by Stoke fouling the ball, but the free kick came to naught. Still pressing, the Villa forced a corner, but although they kept the ball around the Stoke goal, there was no sting about the finishing efforts. Stoke's right wing put in a good run and centre, but the effort was futile, and a moment later Latham effected a clever save when Wheldon was rushing upon him. Spencer was then seen to advantage in tackling Schofield, and another temporary stoppage ensued as one of the Stoke men was hurt. From a corner the Villa threatened without result and Wilkes had to run out at the other end. Hereabouts the play dragged somewhat, little combination being observable on either side. Devey got clear away, but missed his mark with a long shot. From a free kick the visitors got away, and a good swinging centre being sent across from the right, Baird and Wood managed to beat

THE ALBION BEAT THE CHAMPIONS

● The sensation of Saturday afternoon's matches was, of course, the downfall of Aston Villa at West Bromwich. Although it was generally recognised that the Albion had greatly strengthened their team since last season, no one for a moment expected that they would prove equal to the task of overthrowing the League Champions. Yet they managed it, and right well did they deserve their triumph, too. The expensive Villa team – including the two players whose transfer cost the club some £600, Wheldon and Whitehouse – had much the best of the first half, but after the interval several of the men tired perceptibly, and the home forwards, seeing their opportunity, did not fail to take full advantage of it. The Villa backs are not a brilliant pair by any means, and they were unable to stand the strain of the Albion attack for long, and the result of the game was a victory for the wooden spoonists of last year by 3 goals to 1.

FLESH ON THE VILLA

● There are at least four of the Villa players who have far too much flesh on them to play for an hour and a half without tiring greatly. These are Campbell, Devey, Welford and Reynolds; a week's hard training would do them a world of good.

WHERE WILL WHELDON PLAY?

● The Villa forward line is composed of five of the most brilliant players in the kingdom, and when the men have settled down, the attack will want such a lot of stopping. It is questionable, however, if Wheldon will play as well on the right wing as on the left. It is by no means unlikely that the ex-Heathen will be moved to the left wing to partner John Cowan. Devey and Athersmith, playing together, form the best right wing in the country, and the genial 'Mac' is not alone in his opinion.

FRED WHELDON

BRIEFLETS...

☞ *George Russell, the old Aston Villa half-back, is playing for Gravesend United. The Southerners evidently have a liking for Aston Villa players, as four others – Cox, Price, Podmore and Louis Campbell – are now connected with their club.*

☞ *The German footballers who visited the south of England last week have returned home. Their record was: Played 4, lost 4; goals for 0, against 45. What a magnificent record.*

☞ *Evans was sick during the Albion match. Many of the Villa were sick after it.*

'BEST MEN' BEATEN

● There has been wailing and gnashing of teeth in local football circles this week, for has not the team of internationals and two hundred guinea men been handsomely beaten by the despised and cheap combination of Black Country lads who now wear the colours of West Bromwich Albion? Remembering how loudly the policy of 'the best men at any price' was so continuously and boastfully proclaimed in the spring, and was carried out in style that made the hair of the old-fashioned managers of teams stand on end, it is a little singular that the result of so much scattered treasure should be two inglorious displays as we have so far been favoured with.

Wilkes between them, and put on Stoke's first goal. The home players were soon attacking again, John Cowan missing the goal by a foot or two only, whilst Athersmith was cheered for a good shot. Latham effected a fine save from a lightning shot, but the visitors found themselves driven into goal after time.

Charlie Athersmith

The last few minutes were exciting as the Villa bore down again, but again a visiting player was hurt. There was nothing serious about it and play continued in a bad light until the final whistle blew with the score: Villa 2 goals, Stoke 1.

Aston Villa: Wilkes; Welford and Spencer; Crabtree, Cowan and Reynolds; Athersmith, Wheldon, Devey, Cowan and Campbell.

Stoke: Latham; Eccles and Clare; Dickson, Simpson and Brodie; Johnson, Maxwell, Baird, Wood and Schofield.

LEAGUE DIVISION ONE
Saturday 5th September, 1896
ALBION 3, VILLA 1

● The opening match of the season at Stoney Lane between the Villa and the Albion attracted about 12,000 spectators, notwithstanding the fact the rain fell the whole afternoon. Devey won the toss and set the Albion to kick down hill the first half with the wind in their faces.

The opening exchanges were of a give and take character, the leather frequently being sent outside. Williams checked Campbell and Spencer stopped the career of Garfield. At length the ball was soon cannoning from head to head in front of the Albion goal, Williams conceding a corner to get rid of it. The leather was placed behind from the flag kick, and Bassett and McLeod next skipped away together, only to have their career cut short by Crabtree. Free kicks for trivial offences became frequent and from one of these Athersmith got possession, sending in a lovely centre, but Campbell shot wide. The game was fast and exciting but neither team threatened goal seriously. The Villa forwards were responsible for some clever passing but they had to shoot at long distances so that Reader dealt effectively with them. McLeod started down the centre, and the ball went to and from Bassett and McLeod, Crabtree ultimately dispossessing them. From a free kick splendidly placed by Williams, Higgins had a shy at goal, but Richards spoilt the chance by getting offside. Devey and Wheldon both sent hard shots for Reader to negotiate, and Campbell ended a dangerous attack by kicking wide. Devey got through the Albion backs but shot at long distance, Reader making a very clever save. At length the Villa were rewarded, the ball going from left to right, Athersmith touching to Wheldon, and the latter to the centre, when Devey with a fine shot scored the first goal. The Villa played with great confidence afterwards and a long shot by Campbell was only partially stopped by Reader, Williams darting up in the nick of time and saving. The Albion made one or two good efforts, but the interval arrived with the score standing: Villa 1, Albion 0.

Crossing over Devey sent down the centre, and Wheldon banged in a magnificent shot which Reader cleverly handled. Williams took a free kick in midfield and sent through without a second player touching it. The Albion began to shape better than in the first half but the Villa backs were playing a great game and successfully dealt with all their efforts. Athersmith and Wheldon were stopped again and again by Williams, whose back play was one of the features of the match. John Cowan and Campbell made a speedy effort but Evans checked them, and Garfield raced away up the left. His centre went right across the goalmouth and Bassett found the wrong side of the post. Ford tried a long shot which Whitehouse cleared at the expense of a corner. This was cleared but Bassett made several speedy runs, and a couple of fruitless corners followed.

Dear Sir...

● Being a constant reader of your valuable paper, I should be glad if you will kindly insert the following:- Having witnessed the last two League matches of this club, both away and at home, I and my colleagues have come to the conclusion that something ought to be done at once in replacing and rearranging the front rank, and we should like to suggest that one who is much too slow for a team like the Villa should be left out. We do not lose sight of the fact that this player can shoot, but what is the use of his shooting powers if he can't get in a position to shoot? I noticed on Saturday last the ball was passed to him continually, but he was robbed of it just as often. We all know the Villa are a club who can get good players. In the trial matches at Perry Barr several youths showed good form, especially Harris, who played centre in the fourth trial. Then we say why not give these young ones a chance? –
Yours, &c., VILLA FOLLOWERS,
Florence Road, Smethwick.

Dismal disappointment

● After all the boasting during the summer of how no expense had been spared to strengthen the team, and that the League Championship and English Cups would both be gained during the present season, the doings of Aston Villa have so far been a dismal disappointment to their supporters. Of course it is much too early in the year to judge of the merits of the respective clubs, but it is quite certain that unless the Villa show greatly improved form during the next few weeks their chance of again becoming League Champions will have vanished entirely.

Poor exhibition by the Villa

● The Villa v Sheffield United game was a very uninteresting affair, and the five thousand spectators assembled were very disappointed at the poor exhibition of the home team. Of course the absence of Welford, and the consequent reorganisation of the team, may partly account for this, but the forwards have showed very little of last year's form, while at half-back James Cowan seems to have deteriorated somewhat. In the second half of the game the Villa forward line was altered, in the manner suggested in my notes last week, Wheldon going from inside right to inside left, Campbell being put in the centre, and Devey partnering Athersmith on the right. The men played much better in their new positions, and it is to be hoped that they will be allowed to retain them.

Policy which never pays

● 'Chopping and changing' is a policy which never pays, and yet the Villa have been represented by a different eleven in each of the five games in which they have taken part this season. The following is a list of goal-getters up to date: Wheldon 5, Devey 2, Crabtree, John Cowan, Welford and Burton 1 each.

Excursion to Everton

● Tomorrow the Villa visit Everton to oppose the present leaders of the League, and they will have to be in remarkably fine trim if they are going to prove victorious, for the 'Toffee Merchants' are going very strongly. Mr W. McGregor has arranged a cheap half-day excursion from Birmingham to Liverpool – return fare three shillings – and there will doubtless be a big crowd of Villa enthusiasts at Goodison Park to cheer their favourites. The Astonians have never won a match on this ground, and they will be fortunate if they escape defeat tomorrow: still, the game should be well worth witnessing, and the McGregor excursion should be well patronised.

The Albion were playing a plucky game and after a time Bassett planted the leather in goal, almost from the cornerflag. The other forwards made a rush and Garfield safely landed it in the net. After this the game was faster than ever, the Villa awakening to the seriousness of the position, and the Albion exhibiting great pluck and determination. The home forwards went for goal in a bunch and Welford fouled. The referee awarded a penalty kick which was entrusted to Williams, who safely put it through the posts. The complexion of the game had been totally changed in the course of a few minutes and the Albion were now playing a great game. McLeod started up the centre and got the better of Welford. Garfield seized on the ball, and after taking a few paces forward he shot paced Whitehouse with a splendid shot. With only a few minutes to play victory was now assured, and nothing further of interest happening, the result was: Albion 3, Villa 1.

West Bromwich Albion: Reader; Evans and Williams; T. Perry, Higgins and Banks; Bassett, McLeod, Ford, Richards and Garfield.

Aston Villa: Whitehouse; Spencer and Welford; Reynolds, Cowan and Crabtree; Athersmith, Wheldon, Devey, Campbell and John Cowan.

DIVISION ONE	P	W	L	D	F	A	Pt
West Brom. Albion	2	2	0	0	5	2	4
Everton	2	2	0	0	3	1	4
Nottingham Forest	2	1	0	1	5	1	3
Preston North End	2	1	0	1	5	3	3
Sheffield United	2	1	0	1	3	2	3
Bury	2	1	0	1	1	0	3
Sheffield Wednesday	2	1	1	0	4	3	2
Liverpool	2	1	1	0	2	2	2
Blackburn Rovers	2	1	1	0	2	2	2
Wolverhampton Wan.	2	1	1	0	2	2	2
Bolton Wanderers	2	0	2	0	1	1	2
Aston Villa	2	1	0	1	3	4	2
Stoke	2	1	1	0	2	5	2
Sunderland	2	0	1	1	1	2	1
Derby County	2	0	1	1	1	2	1
Burnley	2	0	1	1	1	2	1

FRIENDLY MATCH

Thursday 10th September 1896

Grimsby Town 3, Villa 3

● This match was played at the Abbey Park Ground, Grimsby, last evening in beautiful weather and before some 4,000 spectators, local interest running high from the fact, in addition to the reputation of the visitors, that the match was a benefit one for the home team following the transfer of Whitehouse.

It was the Villans first appearance at Grimsby, and they were heartily welcomed, Whitehouse especially receiving an ovation. the visitors won the toss and played from the Park goal, facing a light breeze. From the kick off the ball was immediately taken by Evans. Give-and-take play followed, and a foul in goal was given in favour of the Villans. The fishermen, however, managed to get the ball away, and for a time both goalkeepers were kept fairly busy in turn, but ultimately Whitehouse was beaten, Rodgers scoring the first goal for Grimsby after about 10 minutes' play. Aston Villa equalised from a scrimmage, the half time score thus being – Grimsby Town, 1 goal; Aston Villa, 1 goal.

JOTTINGS AT THE
ASTON VILLA v.
SHEFFIELD UNITED.

CERTAIN FORM
Athersmith

A BRILLIANT
SAVE BY WILKES

A SHOT BY DEVEY

WHEN THE VILLA SCORED

THE DEFENCE
OF FOULKES

REYNOLDS HEADING
THE BALL JUST OVER
THE BAR

18 SEPTEMBER 1896

A LUCKY MAN

● John Devey, the Villa Captain, is a lucky man; not only has he played football longer than most of us can remember the game, with a skill that has secured him immunity from those serious accidents which befall to the lot of so many fine players, but his benefit falls due at a time when shilling subscriptions have become fashionable, and as he is, or has been, connected with nearly every branch of sport in the Midlands, he may confidently hope to receive a sum larger than has ever rewarded the lot of a Birmingham footballer before. As he still a young man he may reasonably expect to fill his present onerous position a few years longer before he takes with him into retirement the good wishes, and we sincerely hope, something more satisfying, of numerous admirers.

When play was resumed the Villa for a long time kept the ball well in the home quarters, but ultimately Grimsby broke away, and would have scored from a scrimmage but for Whitehouse's fine goalkeeping. McCairns finally doubled Grimsby's score, this being quickly followed by another point, notched by Rodgers. The visitors now played for all they were worth, and succeeded in adding 2 more goals to their score, the game thus resulting in a draw – Grimsby, 3 goals; Aston Villa, 3 goals.

Grimsby: Wallace; Lindsey and Davis; Munn, Chapman and Graham; Rodgers, Morris, McCairns, Fletcher and Hogan.

Aston Villa: Whitehouse; Evans and Welford; Chatt, Cowan and Crabtree; Athersmith, Wheldon, Devey, Campbell and Smith.

Saturday 12th September 1896
VILLA 2, SHEFFIELD UTD 2

● There were not more than 5,000 spectators at Perry Barr on Saturday to witness the start of the game between these clubs, the weather being dull and showery. In deference to the wishes of the Cycle Parade executive, the kick-off was much earlier than usual, three o'clock seeing the game started.

Owing to some little hitch, Welford and Whitehouse were left out of the team, Wilkes and Burton being again called upon. Considering the heavy rain, the players were enabled to obtain a capital footing, and playing towards the entrance goal at the commencement, the Villa backs were at once called upon to repress an aggressive movement by the visiting forwards, who got off at a rare pace. Then the Villa bore down upon the Sheffield goal in turn, Foulkes thus early putting in good work. Not to be beaten back easily, the home side kept the fight well in opposition quarters, but the pressure ceased when the ball was headed over. For a time there was little to choose between the sides, play being confined to midfield, but the referee was pretty strict on fouls, and the Villa getting the worst of these decisions had their work cut out to keep Sheffield back. Once near goal the visitors showed great persistency, and after the ball had been worked around the home posts, Henderson put the finishing touch to some strenuous work by planting it into the net. Fairly roused by this reverse, the Villa men got down to the visitors' goal in good style, and twice Foulkes saved his charge most skillfully. Not to be denied, the forwards rattled in again, and a corner kick falling to the Villa, Burton put his side on equal terms with a capital shot. Campbell showed up with a

Johnny Campbell

fine attempt, but Foulkes was very safe, although a little later he should have been easily beaten by Wheldon, who missed a palpable opening. Devey and Campbell both put in slashing work, but could not meet with any success in shooting for goal. From a free kick, Crabtree apparently scored, the ball seeming to hit John Cowan before going into the net. The referee, however, negatived the appeal, and the interval arrived with the score one goal each.

A fast sprint by Athersmith was followed up with a good centre, and Foulkes was early called into action. He quickly cleared, but returning to the siege the Villa kept him employed, his keeping during a hot time being really fine. Yates and Henderson got away at length, but Crabtree's defence proved sound, and the Villa came swinging back at a good pace, only for John Cowan to miss an easy chance of scoring. Devey changed places with Wheldon, who went on the left wing, Campbell taking the centre. This worked well at once, a second goal falling to the Villa from a beautiful bit of forward work, Wheldon heading the ball into the net from Athersmith's centre. The United then retaliated, but the whistle had been blown for a foul just

OLD VILLANS RETURN WITH BERWICK

● Berwick Rangers will be at Perry Barr tomorrow, playing against Aston Villa Reserves in the Birmingham League competition. The Rangers' team includes three erstwhile Villans, Benwell, Purslow, and Albert Brown, so their visit should be productive of more than usual interest.

FOOTBALL FEVER

● How these football legislators love one another! Mr. Louis Ford, of the Albion, has just been giving a dinner to celebrate his victory over Mr J. Whitehouse of the Villa, as a midland representative on the Council of the Football Association, and greatly deplored that the indignity of begging for votes from the little clubs should have been put on him after eight years service, but we fail to discover any reason in his speech why his office should be retained for life. A man may reasonably rejoice on winning a flight but it is the height of absurdity to suggest that he should never be opposed. This office has of course no pay attached to it, and outsiders will wonder at the eagerness with which it – like other honorary distinctions in the football world – is sought after, and the bitterness aroused between the rival candidates, but I am afraid their curiosity will not be satisfied until the publication of a little book called 'The Privileges of Football Committee Men,' which a friend of ours who has been connected with the game in this district for many years, is understood to be preparing. This will elucidate many points which have puzzled votaries of the game, and we predict a warm welcome for it from all those people 'who want to know, you know.'

OVERNIGHT STOP

● Darwen have sent in a claim to Small Heath for their hotel expenses last Monday, as the kick-off was fixed too late for them to get home the same evening. The matter is to be brought before the League. As Small Heath gave them a Monday for a Saturday match, the claim is somewhat unreasonable.

BRIEFLETS...

∞ Many people preferred witnessing the Cycle Parade to the Sheffield United v Villa match last week. They were wise.

∞ Aston Villa have not as yet arranged to meet any Scotch clubs this season. If they could get the Celtic club to visit Perry Barr during the next month or so, a good 'gate' would be a certainty.

THE CRITIC...

∞ Oh, if the Villa forwards would only stop that stupid practice of fiddling about in front of goal! Outsiders are poking fun at the Villa.

∞ Fred Burton was not as sprightly as usual against the United.

∞ Crabtree is about the only man in the Villa team who is really playing his game this season.

∞ It wouldn't be wise to back 'Jamie' Cowan to win an Edinburgh handicap in his present form.

James Crabtree

∞ The Villa supporters are quite elated, and some of them think their pets are going to lick creation. Umph!

∞ 'Mac' was mightily incensed when those blockheads of gatekeepers at Everton wouldn't let him in.

William McGregor

before the ball went into the goal. Play now became a bit scratchy, and after Henderson had recovered from a slight injury, the Sheffielders began to force the pace. A long return by Cain into the Villa goal found Wilkes at his best, but from the corner kick which followed his tipping the ball over the bar, Priest scored for the United, the scores again being levelled. Towards the close the Villa made desperate efforts to obtain a lead, but without effect, Campbell failing when a good chance presented itself. Foulkes did work right to the finish, when the score remained:- Villa, 2 goals; Sheffield United, 2.

Aston Villa: Wilkes; Spencer and Crabtree; Reynolds, James Cowan and Burton; Athersmith, Wheldon, Devey, Campbell and John Cowan.

Sheffield United: Foulkes; Whittam and Cain; Howell, Morren and Needham,; Yates, Henderson, Walls, Needham and Priest.

LEAGUE DIVISION ONE

Saturday 19th September 1896
EVERTON 2, VILLA 3

● A tremendous crowd of some 20,000 assembled at Goodison Park to witness this match, about 1,000 of these having travelled from Birmingham to the head-quarters of the Everton Football Club. The weather was beautifully fine when the game started, at four o'clock, but before the interval arrived a tremendous rainstorm burst over the district, the players being drenched to the skin in a few moments.

For once in a way the Villa team were seen to great advantage, the improvement being most noticeable in the front division, all the forwards playing in much more resolute style than hitherto this season. Taking the lead in the first few minutes, they got further ahead before half-time, and although once or twice in the second half Everton looked like getting level, they failed to make up lost ground, and eventually suffered defeat by 3 goals to 2, a result thoroughly warranted by the play. Mr. Lewis had the men on the mark in good time, and no sooner had the struggle opened than Everton got away, only to be promptly decked by Spencer. Having made the pace a cracker, the Villa responded in like fashion, the ball travelling swiftly from end to end. The sharp work of the forwards on the Villa side was backed up by resolute tackling by the halves, Reynolds being conspicuous early in the game. Travelling up to goal in pretty style, the Villa found an opening, and Devey promptly put the ball into the net only a few moments from the start. This success meant a deal for the Villa, who worked with refreshing brisk-ness. Everton, too, played a dashing game, Whitehouse in goal saving brilliantly from Cameron, Bell, and Chadwick, the home forwards taking shots at long ranges whenever there was a chance. Devey and Athersmith did splendid work together, and their efforts were well supported by the opposite wing, John Cowan showing fine speed against Barker, fairly out-pacing him time after time. After several long shots from the right had been dealt with, the Villa men closed in again, and Campbell fairly surprised the goal-keeper with a sudden shot into the net. Soon after this rain commenced to fall in torrents, and long kicking by the half-backs and backs was indulged in chiefly, skill-ful passing or running being well-nigh impossible under the conditions. When the interval came round the Villa were leading by 2 goals to 0.

The change of costumes by both teams must have been very welcome, and by the time the men were on the field again the sun was shining brilliantly, but it was easy to see that the sun had made the going very slippery. Everton's right-wing pair were soon promi-nent on restarting, but Crabtree was playing a master-ly game at back, and Bell found it difficult to pass him. In a tussle for the ball near the Villa goal-line James Cowan was penalised for a foul. This was taken very prettily by Stewart, who lifted the ball clean from the left wing to the right, and Taylor had little trouble in heading it into the goal. There was much cheering, but

SNAIL RAIL

● Over a thousand Villa enthusiasts travelled by the McGregor excursion to Liverpool to witness the match, and a right royal time they had of it, too! Of course the train was late reaching its destination, and by the time the excursionists reached Goodison Park, the game had been in progress 15 minutes, and the Villa were a goal to the good. How is it that these excursions never arrive punctually?

WHO'S GRUMBLING NOW?

● Previous to Saturday, the Villa had never won a game at Everton, and their victory was all the more popular on this account. Compared with last season's results, Aston Villa are now one point to the good, having lost one at West Bromwich and gained two at Everton. And yet it was only a week ago that everyone was grumbling at their poor performances!

DESERVING OF SUPPORT

● The John Devey Testimonial Fund deserves the support of every genuine football enthusiast in the district. Everyone should contribute to it – even if it is only a shilling that you can afford. Why? Well, here are half-a-dozen reasons, which I cull from a correspondent's letter to a contemporary:
(1) Because through his long and distinguished career he has maintained an untarnished reputation.
(2) Because his play has been so consistent and good that no football club for whom he has played has ever placed him in the reserve team.
(3) Because his excellent conduct, both on and off the field, has done much to elevate professional football.
(4) Because during his captaincy Aston Villa have reached a pinnacle of fame never before accomplished, inasmuch as they have won the English Cup once and the League Championship twice.
(5) Because, although a professional cricketer, he has given his splendid services to our leading Birmingham club (Aston Unity) for over 12 years, and has always been one of their brightest stars.
(6) Because he is a Birmingham man by birth and education, and has always striven to do credit to his native town.

2 OCTOBER 1896

FORM DISAPPOINTS

● What a delusion is football 'form'! Those people who expected to see the Villa defeat Everton at Perry Barr on Saturday, because they had beaten them at Goodison Park a week previously – and the writer of these notes was among the number – were sadly disappointed, for although the League Champions had much the best of the play, their forwards never once shaped like getting goals, and it cannot be gainsaid that the Evertonians well deserved their triumph. It was unfortunate that the Villa were without the services of Howard Spencer, whose presence in the team might have made all the difference between losing and winning.

BIRMINGHAM-ON-SEA

● Small Heath will once again be in the First Division of the League! When? When Birmingham's a seaport city; at least that is the general opinion if they do not greatly improve upon their display against Lincoln City last week.

the Villa were soon on the attack again, Campbell being pushed from behind, with the goal at his mercy. John Cowan again fastened on it, and this time Campbell made no mistake, for he beat Briggs with a rare, clean shot. This success had its effect on the home side for a time, but, bracing themselves up, they got into a swing again, and Millward scored again with a wonderful screw shot from near the corner flag. Whitehouse being completely beaten by the flight of the ball. Cheered on most enthusiastically by the supporters, the Everton men made the most gallant efforts to get on equal terms, but the Villa team kept their heads through a rather trying time, and gradually drove their opponents into their own goal. Right up to the finish the play was most interesting, but no more scoring was done, the Villa gaining a meritorious victory by 3 goals to 2.

Aston Villa: Whitehouse; Spencer and Crabtree; Reynolds, James Cowan and Burton; Athersmith, Devey, Campbell, Wheldon and John Cowan.

Everton: Briggs; Storris and Barker; Boyle, Holt and Stewart; Bell, Taylor, Cameron, Chadwick and Millward.

● At Leicester yesterday in wet weather, before 2,000 spectators. In the first half the Fosse made a very good show, and at the interval the Villa had only 1 goal to brag of the score. The game was exceedingly well contested during the second stage of the play considering the greasy state of the ground, and was much better than could have been anticipated. Result: Aston Villa 3 goals, Leicester 2.

● As might have been expected from their fine performance at Liverpool a week ago, there was a large gathering of Villa supporters at Perry Barr on Saturday, when the return match between the Villa and Everton was played. There were quite 20,000 spectators present, and as the weather cleared just before the start, the match was played under favourable circumstances, except, perhaps, that the turf was a little too much on the soft side.

Both clubs were well represented, Arridge appearing vice Barker in the back division, and Hartley superceding Cameron as centre forward on the visiting side; whilst, owing to a domestic affliction, Spencer was unable to play for the Villa, and Welford reappeared, Crabtree partnering him, and Burton occupying the left-half-back position. Everton won the toss, and played with the wind, hill, and sun in their favour, but on settling down after the opening exchanges the Villa were the first to threaten danger. From a free kick Welford placed the ball well, but Reynolds kicked out. A push by Athersmith gave the visitors an opening from the foul, but it was not utilised, and, the Villa going to the other end, John Cowan and Campbell fired good shots, which were cleared cleverly by Briggs and Arridge. After an unproductive corner to Everton, Welford stopped a strong attack, and then breaking away again, Devey went right through his opponents and scored a beautiful goal 15 minutes from the start. Scarcely had the cheering died away, however, than the Everton left threatened danger, and after a few passes in close proximity to the home goal,

James Crabtree

THE OMNISCIENT FOOTBALL MANIAC

● I was at Perry Barr on Saturday last and had the misfortune to sit next to one of the most excited football enthusiasts it has ever been my lot to come across. I had heard of 'football maniacs' before, but I never met one until then, and I am confident those other persons who were within hearing distance of this 'enthusiast' in the grand stand will agree with me that his company is not to be sought.

Before the game commenced he began his deadly work: he evidently believed that his special mission in life was to inform his friends – and enemies – of the doings of the various football clubs in the kingdom, and he gave us the life and history of the Everton players free of charge.

His remarks were intended for his son, a boy of about seven years of age, but as he spoke in a loud tone of voice, it was impossible to miss the stock of stale information which he reeled off. And such information it was, too! If only the compiler of the *Gazette* football guide had been present, he would have been able to take enough notes from this man's conversation to fill his next edition.

We were told that Briggs, the Everton goal-keeper was the Lancashire bowler, and that he had only commenced to play football this season, that Storrier was the Derbyshire wicket-keeper (he was thinking of Storer), and that the Villa were going to win by half-a-dozen goals. This was before the game started, and we were heartily glad when the teams appeared on the ground, being hopeful that the enthusiast would draw his remarks to a close, and confine his attention to the game.

He evidently meant to do no such thing, having made up his mind that his son required a great deal of football knowledge, and we unfortunate people near him were kept in misery the whole afternoon.

When the game started he commenced to adversely criticise the Villa players, and every few minutes we were told that "Reynolds is no good – no judgement whatever," "Welford is a dead frost – what the committee play him for is a mystery to me," "Wheldon's asleep," "Campbell's too slow," "Devey has always been an over-rated man," "Burton only gets his position through favouritism," and numerous other ridiculous remarks. It was sickening to hear his complaints.

One young man asked him why he didn't go on the field to show them how to play, but the remark was treated with silent contempt by the enthusiast, who rattled on as fast as ever.

Towards the close of the match, when Everton had scored their second goal, he remarked that "anybody with a bit of sense could see that the match was sold, as there was not one man trying." Well, it certainly would require a person with a bit of sense to see that – a very little bit of sense, too; in fact, folks with no sense at all could see it clearer still. There was no doubt that he could see it clearly.

It was some relief when the finish came, for if the enthusiast had talked much longer his listeners would have become crazy. The next time I go to Perry Barr I shall keep a good look-out for that enthusiast, and get as far away from him as possible.

'SKY BLUE AND CLARET' EXCURSION TO SHEFFIELD

● An excursion will be run from Birmingham to Sheffield to enable Villa enthusiasts to witness the match tomorrow, and there should be a good number of Brums on the ground to cheer the wearers of the 'sky blue and claret' on to victory – if that desirable result is to be achieved. The Villa have never yet beaten the United in a League match at Bramall Lane; if every man is determined to do his best their run of ill-luck ought to be broken tomorrow.

Welford made the score level by miskicking into his own net. Even play followed, each goal being visited in turn, but the shooting was not very deadly, and the rival goalkeepers were equal to the demands upon them. A fine run and centre by John Cowan should have been utilised, but Athersmith shot over the bar, and though the Villa attacked strongly Briggs saved in brilliant style. John Cowan missed a fine opening, and at the other end Hartley sent in a beauty, which just skimmed the bar. Again Briggs had to fist out with his opponents on him, but he was equal to the occasion, and the interval arrived with the score one goal each.

In the second half, especially during the earlier portion, the Villa had much the best of the play, and were continually attacking. Their final efforts, however, were lacking in dash and precision, and they were met by some splendid defence on the part of Storrier, Arridge, and Briggs. Several shots were fired at long ranges by Wheldon and Campbell, but Briggs had plenty of time to clear them, and was only seldom hard pressed. He had a little anxiety from three successive corners well placed, but even admitting a little luck, he successfully negotiated them, for though the ball was once forced through, it was held to be off-side, and the point was not allowed. John Cowan was several time sadly at fault with goal openings, and seemed unable to get in an accurate centre. When Everton got away they were generally dangerous, and as the result of one burst Taylor got clean away and passed nicely to Chadwick, who with a lovely shot, which gave Whitehouse no chance, put Everton ahead. After this the Villa made desperate efforts to get on terms, but they were unable to do so, and Everton won by 2 goals to 1.

Everton: Briggs; Storrier and Arridge; Boyle, Holt, and Stewart; Bell, Taylor, Hartley, Chadwick and Millward.

Aston Villa: Whitehouse; Crabtree and Welford; Reynolds, James Cowan and Burton; Athersmith, Devey, Campbell, Wheldon and John Cowan.

Pride of Warwickshire

● Although the Villa were beaten (by Everton), there is nothing at all to be ashamed of, and if they continue to play as well throughout the season as they did on Saturday, the club ought again to secure the League Championship. A lot of people blame Welford for the defeat, but this is manifestly unfair, for although it cannot be denied that he was mainly responsible for Everton's first goal, it must be remembered that he was playing in a position which he had never previously occupied. When he and Crabtree changed places, the 'pride of Warwickshire'

JAMES WELFORD

showed up at his best, and Bell and Taylor seldom had a look in. The best teams cannot always win, and it is no use grumbling; the Villa accomplished a fine performance at Everton, and the 'Toffy Merchants' did ditto at Perry Barr. Yet some folks are never satisfied.

Derby for Devey

● On Monday next Jack Devey, the highly-respected Aston Villa skipper, takes a well-deserved benefit, Derby County opposing the League Champions at Perry Barr. There is no more deserving player in the kingdom, and it is to be hoped that there will be an attendance worthy of the occasion.

Nothing in Reserve

● Aston Villa Reserves are a poor lot this season. Their forward line is probably the weakest in the Birmingham League, although Steve Smith is amongst them. The little international is, of course, streets ahead of his four comrades, and it is hard on Smith that he should be compelled to play in such company. The defence is all right, but the Villa Reserves will not win the Championship this year.

Blades blunted

● Aston Villa did not fare at all badly at Bramall Lane on Saturday. True, they only succeeded in gaining a single point, but as they had never previously escaped defeat in a League match there, the result was quite satisfactory.

No worse

● The Villa are not one whit worse off this season than they were last. They have only gained six points out of six matches, but they fared in a similar manner last year, and yet finished at the head of the League. Some folks are never contented. What would Small Heath not give to be in the Villa's shoes today?

Golden goals

● One 'genius' wrote to the papers last week suggesting that the Villa Committee should offer the players talent money for each goal they scored in League matches, in order to encourage them to shoot for goal oftener. He apparently forgets that combination among forwards is an absolute necessity if games are to be won with anything like regularity, and that, if his suggestion were carried out, there would be no combination whatever, as each player would work for his own hand. What wiseacres these anonymous football correspondents are, to be sure!

Brieflet...

☞ *Aston Villa have arranged to play a match at Stoke on Monday, November 30th, for Billy Dickson's benefit.*

● The return match between these clubs was played on the ground of the former at Bramall Lane in the presence of some 10,000 or 12,000 persons, including a fair proportion of Birmingham enthusiasts, who availed themselves of the Midland excursion, and arrived on the scene in excellent time.

Both sides were fully representative. The ground, owing to the recent rains, was on the heavy side. The United won the toss and played with a slight breeze at their backs. They started with much more spirit than the Villa, and had considerably the best of the opening exchanges. Indeed, the visiting backs and goalkeeper were kept busily employed, and had there been any cleverness and resource amongst the Sheffield forwards they must have scored more than once. Early on there was a tendency to roughness on both sides, and fouls were most frequent. Needham played a splendid game against Devey and Athersmith, and the right wing were seldom allowed to become dangerous. On the other hand, Burton was scarcely a match for Yates and Henderson, and as a consequence Crabtree was kept continually on the go. Repeatedly the United got through the visitors' backs, but their final efforts were very tame, and frequently they were spoiled for the outside men lying offside or by fouls for which there was not the least excuse. A couple of free kicks to the Villa gave them an opportunity, but Reynolds shot over the bar, and Wheldon missed badly. At the other end Whitehouse was lucky to save from Henderson, and then the Villa playing a little better pressed awhile, but both Athersmith and Campbell shot in the tamest fashion. A fine run by Devey was spoiled by Cowan getting offside, but they attacked again from a foul, and the home goal had a very lucky escape, the ball on one occasion striking the bar. United then had the best of the play up to the interval, but failed to score, the teams crossing over without a point having been scored.

Fred Burton

The later stage of the game found the Villa as much the aggressors as the home side had been in the first half, but here again they failed to take advantage of their openings. Athersmith made a couple of fine runs, and got in excellent centres, but they were unaccountably missed by his comrades, and from another cross shot by Wheldon which passed right in front of the goal Devey and Campbell had a grand chance, but let it slide. Occasionally the United forwards got away, but the defence proved equal to their by no means brilliant efforts. At its best, though, the kicking of the Villa backs and half-backs was not of the strongest. Once Whitehouse was very lucky, for he entirely misjudged the ball, and Henderson breasted it just outside the posts. Athersmith went off with another dash, and got past the United backs, but his final shot, a long one, was very wide of the mark. On one occasion Foulkes was allowed to run the ball a long way past the half-way line before parting with it, and after Wheldon had headed over the bar from a lovely centre by Athersmith, the same player narrowly escaped scoring with a fast shot which Foulkes was fortunate to save. The Villa had a shade the best of it to the finish, but failed to score, and the game ended in a draw with no goals.

Sheffield United: Foulkes; Witham and Cain; Howell, Morren and Needham; Yates, Henderson, Almond, Hammond and Priest.

Aston Villa: Whitehouse; Spencer and Crabtree, backs; Reynolds, James Cowan and Burton; Athersmith, Devey, Campbell, Wheldon and John Cowan.

HODGETTS TRANSFERRED TO SMALL HEATH

● For some time past Small Heath have been feeling the want of a capable left-wing forward, therefore, when it became known that there was a possibility of securing the services of Dennis Hodgetts, who has rendered such brilliant service to Aston Villa in the past, the directors quickly bestirred themselves to secure his transfer. The negotiations were satisfactorily concluded on Saturday morning, when all the necessary forms were signed, and it is expected that Hodgetts will turn out at Coventry Road on Saturday next against Gainsborough Trinity. His experience and excellent knowledge of the game should make him a most valuable recruit among the youngsters of the Small Heath team.

DENNIS HODGETTS

JUST TOO MUCH

● Poor Small Heath! The glory of the Coventry Road team has indeed departed, their two successive League defeats on their own ground having disheartened hundreds of their supporters. Had they been beaten by any of the top-sawyers of the League, their failures could have been forgiven; but to allow two such clubs as Lincoln City and Burton Swifts to lower their colours in view of their own supporters – well, it is too much for those who desire to see the club regain a position in the First Division of the League to stand.

RAIN SPOILS PAY-DAY

● It was a pity rain spoilt Devey's benefit match, for, on a fine day, the game would have attracted sufficient spectators to make it worth while playing, though after the experience spectators have had of friendly matches at Perry Barr, it would be absurd to expect an attendance which would give a player an adequate reward for all his years of service. Happily, however, Devey's friends have worked hard on his behalf, and there is no reason to doubt that he will receive more than £100, which is about the usual amount derived from a Villa benefit. Of the game little need be said; there was no need for the players to exert themselves, and they didn't. It proves conclusively, however, that Smith is not now fit for the first team, and that Chatt is by no means a terror. Evans, the new back is, we should say, a decided acquisition. In view of the match with the Albion tomorrow training rules have been strictly enforced during the week, and a great effort is to be made to win another match at home.

NEW VILLA BADGE

● Tom Horton, one of the Old Villans – and a good one, too! – has brought out a new football badge. It is in the form of a shield and the one we saw represented Aston Villa. It is beautifully enamelled in colours on brass, is retailed at sixpence, and is sure to become extremely popular. The badge can be worn in coat or hat, and makes an extremely pretty ornament – much superior to the gimcrack arrangements we have been used to. All the League clubs are to be honoured in the same way.

DIVISION ONE	P	W	L	D	F	A	Pt
Bolton Wanderers	4	2	0	2	6	3	6
Liverpool	5	3	2	0	6	5	6
Sheffield United	3	2	0	1	6	2	5
Blackburn Rovers	4	2	1	1	6	2	5
West Brom. Albion	4	2	1	1	7	6	5
Aston Villa	4	2	1	1	8	8	5
Notts Forest	3	1	0	2	7	3	4
Preston North End	3	1	0	2	6	4	4
Everton	3	2	1	0	5	4	4
Burnley	4	1	1	2	4	4	4
Bury	4	1	2	1	2	3	3
Derby County	4	1	2	1	5	7	3
Wolverhampton Wan.	4	1	3	0	5	7	2
Sheffield Wednesday	4	1	3	0	5	9	2
Stoke	4	1	3	0	5	10	2
Sunderland	5	0	3	2	5	11	2

JOHN DEVEY BENEFIT MATCH

Monday 5th October 1896
VILLA 2, DERBY COUNTY 1

● A friendly match between these clubs was played yesterday at Perry Barr for the benefit of John Devey, who since 1891 has been one of the leading players in the Villa team. Unfortunately the weather was very unfavourable, and there were not more than 2,000 spectators present, but with his guarantee and subscription list Devey will do very well.

It was intended to try Crabtree centre forward, but owing to injuries received on Saturday he and Reynolds were both out of the Villa team. The Villa won the toss and Derby kicked off up hill. The opening exchanges were fairly evenly divided, the Villa being the first to threaten danger on the left, but Smith's shot, though a good one, was kept out by Robinson. The play was fast, and Derby had none the worst of it, a capital long shot by Stevenson being only just wide. Immediately afterwards Goodall tried a good one, whilst at the other end Devey put the ball to Smith, whose final effort was a few yards wide. A fine attack was made by Wheldon, Devey, and Athersmith, the last-named sending in a good one, which Robinson only half cleared, but though Smith was in attendance with a nice opening he shot wide of the mark. Derby then went off with a rush, and from a pass by Paul, Stevenson had the goal clear, but shot outside. The Villa again attacked, and Wheldon should have got on a pass from Devey, but was a moment too late. A corner to the home team was unproductive, and a brilliant piece of play and a lively shot by Athersmith deserved a better fate than to miss by a few inches only. Directly afterwards Athersmith tried another beauty, which was only saved at the expense of a corner. Nothing came of it, but Devey got away in clever fashion, and finished a splendid effort by shooting a pretty goal. The home side continued to have the best of the play, and after Athersmith had twice missed by the narrowest of shaves John Cowan sent in a grand one, which Robinson just tipped over the bar. The corner was cleared, and Derby went up the field in dashing style, Miller and Fisher both getting in fine shots, that from the former being grandly saved by Whitehouse. Staley hurt himself and had to retire, and Wheldon, getting away smartly, beat Robinson, and scored the second goal in good style. Derby again went up the field, Whitehouse bringing off a couple of clever saves, whilst McQueen missed a clear opening. Athersmith, after a capital effort, put the ball into the net, but he had been fouled before, and, unfortunately, the goal did not count. Nothing came from the free kick, for though Miller handled the ball it escaped the observation of the referee. At half-time the Villa were leading by 2 goals to 0.

On resuming the Villa were the first to attack, and from a nice bit of play by Smith and Wheldon, Robinson brought off a smart save. Still pressing, Wheldon had two good openings, but shot badly each time, and when Derby came down on the right Evans stopped them cleverly. Derby, however, though still with only ten men, played in the pluckiest fashion, and, getting down the field in line, Stevenson finished

ASTON VILLA V. WEST BROMWICH ALBION.

AN ANXIOUS MOMENT FOR READER
WILLIAMS & DEVEY HAVE A TUG OF WAR.

12 OCTOBER 1896

RECORD RECEIPTS

● Records in every sport are being broken daily, and it is not greatly surprising to learn that the attendance at the Villa v Albion match at Perry Barr on Saturday realised £16 more than the previous highest amount taken in a League match on that ground. Well, the Villa have not made any too much money out of their previous engagements this season, and the cash taken on Saturday will come in very handy when they contemplate arranging for the transfer of a famous player at a similar cost to those of Whitehouse and Wheldon.

SHY AT SCORING

● The Villa's display of Saturday was not quite satisfactory, although they defeated the Albion pointless. The shooting of the forwards was absolutely wretched; in the second half, especially, scores of chances were thrown away by reckless shots. Of course, no one expects them to score a goal every time they get the ball in front of the posts, but, on the other hand, there is no reason why they should shoot without any judgement whatever. As they won, the local dailies have not had much to say against them, but it is an unwise policy to overlook glaring faults in a team because they happen to be on the winning side.

GOOD OL' JIMMY

● Everyone was pleased to see Jimmy Welford in such fine trim. He is a good-hearted fellow, and no one was more sorry than the writer that he started the season in the manner he did. However, he is all right again now, and on Saturday he was by far the best back on the field − and that is no slight honour when it is remembered that Williams and Spencer were playing.

a good run by shooting a pretty goal. Stung by this reverse, the Villa played up very hard, the left wing in particular being seen to considerable advantage. Smith was in great form, and made several fine runs and centres, but nothing came of them. Shortly before the finish Smith hurt his leg and left the field, and though the Villa had the best of the exchanges nothing more was scored, the game ending in a win for the Villa by 2 goals to 1.

Derby County: Robinson; Methven and Staley; Turner, Archie Goodall and Kinsey; Paul, Fisher, Miller, Stevenson and McQueen.

Aston Villa: Whitehouse; Spencer and Evans; Chatt, James Cowan, and Burton; Athersmith, Wheldon, Devey, John Cowan and Smith.

<table>
<tr><td>LEAGUE DIVISION ONE</td></tr>
</table>

Saturday 10th October 1896
VILLA 2, ALBION 0

● The return match between these clubs was played at Perry Barr, and as usual when these old opponents meet there was a tremendous crowd, about 15,000 spectators being present.

Both sides were fully representative, and fortunately the weather kept fine until just before the close. The Villa kicked off up hill and against a stiffish breeze, and they were speedily placed on the defensive, Bassett got in a nice centre, but Ford was yards off-side when he shot into the net. Then from a foul Higgins headed right into goal, Whitehouse fisting away. Evans stopped a break-away by the Villa, and Bassett and Ford were just getting dangerous when Welford pulled them up in clever style. The Albion were going great guns, and it was only the fine defence of Crabtree and the backs, especially of Welford, that kept them out. A nice run by the home forwards ended in John Cowan shooting wide, and Reynolds sending the ball over the bar. The Albion were soon dangerous again, but Ford was at fault through being off-side, and at the other end, after Campbell had tried a long one, Reader was lucky in saving a fast, low shot. The Albion made some fine attempts to get through, but found the home defence too good, and the Villa going off with a rush, headed by James Cowan, Wheldon put the finishing touch to a fine piece of play by shooting a brilliant goal. It was a lovely side shot, and gave Reader no chance. This success seemed to put the Villa on good terms with themselves, and they had much more of the play than had hitherto been the case. Williams, however, from a free-kick sent in a beauty, which hit the post and rebounded into play, and after an exciting scrimmage Ford shot outside. Then the Villa went up again, and from a clever passing run Devey centred well and Campbell headed the second goal − a fine bit of play. The Albion, however, were in no sense discouraged by these reverses, and had the best of the play up to the interval, but they could not score, and the Villa crossed over with the useful lead of 2 goals to 0.

In the second half, with the advantage of the hill and wind, the Villa had much the best of the play, and

Albert Evans

it was seldom indeed the Albion became really dangerous, despite several nice runs, especially on the part of Garfield. Bassett was completely overshadowed by Crabtree and Welford, and moreover, did not get quite as much assistance from McLeod as usual. Williams played a fine game in this half, and was splendidly supported by Evans, who is a very promising young back. Higgins, too, got through a tremendous lot of work in effective style, and the result was the Villa, although they did most of the pressing, failed to add to their score. They had many chances, but were a trifle unsteady at the finish, this being especially the case with two beautiful runs by Athersmith and another by John Cowan. Campbell got in one lovely shot, which was well saved by Reader. Nothing more was done, and

SURPRISE, SURPRISE...

● The announcement that Dennis Hodgetts, the veteran Aston Villa left-wing international forward, had been transferred to Small Heath came as a big surprise to everyone. It was generally understood that Hodgetts had finally retired from active participation in the game in which he had become so deservedly famous, but it seems as though he cannot be contented to act the part of a spectator. Although he is scarcely reliable enough for the Villa, who, in order to lose no possible chance of once more gaining the League Championship, cannot find room for players who have passed the meridian of their youth, Dennis ought to be of great service to his new employers, for the Small Heath front rank sadly needs the addition of a little more weight, while as a coach to the other forwards he will be invaluable. The player who is selected to partner Hodgetts will be a lucky individual; if he has got any football in him at all, the ex-Villan will soon make him into a first-class player. Steve Smith, Louis Campbell, and the late Albert Woolley all had a great deal to thank Hodgetts for, for without his assistance they would never have become so famous as they did.

PEAK PREPARATION

● Tomorrow the Villa are due at Derby to play their first League match of the present season with the County, and as the recent performances of the Perry Pets have given the utmost satisfaction to their supporters, it is safe to assert that a large number of local football enthusiasts will patronise the excursions which are announced to be run to the Peak district. It will be within the recollection of everyone that it was at Derby that the Villa were thrown out of the English Cup competition in the first round last season, while a week later a League game between the two clubs resulted in a draw. Derby County have not played up to their form of last season by a long chalk as yet, and are much lower in the League table than the Villa; still, the Birmingham eleven will have a harder task than some of their supporters imagine to improve upon last season's result, although if they play up to their best form they ought to finish on the right side.

WHAT PRICE, DENNY?

● Wheldon's transfer from Small Heath to Aston Villa cost the latter club something like £300. It would be interesting to learn if the Perry Barr club made the Heathens pay anything for the transfer of Hodgetts.

BRIEFLETS...

↪ *James Cowan, Aston Villa's famous centre half-back, celebrates his 28th birthday on Monday next, while James Elliott attains the age of 27 a day later.*

↪ *The Villa and Albion meet once again on Monday next at West Bromwich to decide which club shall enter the second round of the Staffordshire Cup.*

THE CRITIC...

↪ *Some of your men seem to be rather 'flabby', Grierson.*

↪ *Wheldon, you haven't come up to our expectations yet.*

↪ *The Small Heath defence badly needs some new blood. Twenty-four goals in three League matches, and but three in another two, What a remarkable difference!*

↪ *Has 'Mac' received a letter of regret from Everton yet?*

↪ *The editors of daily papers would do football far more good if they shoved the lucubrations of the army of blithering idiots into the waste-paper basket!*

a thoroughly interesting, pleasant, and well-contested game ended in a win for the Villa by 2 goals to 0.

West Bromwich Albion: Reader; Evans and Williams; Perry, Higgins and Banks; Bassett, McLeod, Ford, Watson and Garfield.

Aston Villa: Whitehouse; Spencer and Welford; Reynolds, James Cowan and Crabtree; Athersmith, Devey, Campbell, Wheldon and John Cowan.

LEAGUE DIVISION ONE

Saturday 17th October 1896
DERBY COUNTY 1, VILLA 3

● Some seven or eight thousand spectators assembled on the Derby ground to witness the first League match of the season between Derby County and Aston Villa, but there was nothing like the excitement of last year, when the two clubs were running neck and neck for the championship.

The Villa had up their usual team, but Derby were without John Goodall and Leiper, the latter being replaced by Archie Goodall. From the kick-off the Derby left went down, and almost immediately sent in a grand shot which Whitehouse cleverly cleared, and each side forced an unproductive corner. The pace was very fast, and after Whitehouse had again been called on the Villa nearly scored from a corner, Robinson being lucky to save. Devey made a fine run and centre, but James Cowan shot over the bar, and Campbell, with a nice opening, missed. The Villa were forcing matters, Athersmith getting in a couple of runs and accurate centres, from the latter of which Wheldon scored a pretty goal, but the referee disallowed it for off-side – a bad mistake. Derby then attacked, and forced two corners, but though they made desperate efforts to get through from an exciting scrimmage, the visitors repelled the storm, and, going up field immediately, Robinson brought off a remarkable save from Campbell. Bloomer, who had been well watched by Crabtree, managed to get through, but at the critical moment Welford – who was playing a grand game – knocked him off the ball, which went out yards wide. A pretty passing run by the Villa forwards left the ball with Wheldon, who sent in a straight one which Robinson perhaps might have saved had it not glanced into the net off Goodall. The visitors had thus drawn first blood, but Derby were in no sense disconcerted, and Whitehouse only half clearing a shot from Miller – it was only by a supreme effort that the Villa custodian reached the ball – Bloomer stood with the goal open but missed badly. Directly afterwards Whitehouse brought off a grand save from Bloomer, and then Campbell's shot grazed the Derby cross-bar. A free kick against Spencer resulted in Stevenson making the scores level, and so matters remained up to the interval, when the rivals crossed over with one goal each.

So far there had not been very much between the teams, but during the second half the Villa were seen to great advantage. Derby did not stay the pace, whereas the visitors kept it up right to the finish, and were decidedly cleverer than their opponents. Indeed, it was only the exceedingly fine goalkeeping of Robinson

FINEST SO FAR

● Assisted by the marvellous wisdom of their anonymous advisers and critics, the Villa committee have at length got their team into form, and the display the men gave at Derby is on all hands acknowledged to be the finest they have shown this year. A gratifying feature of it was the form of Welford, whose big kicks and fearless rushes did much to demoralise his opponents – few forwards care to meet a back of fourteen stone – and with Crabtree playing in front of him we do not anticipate much trouble from any right wing in the League. But the great improvement was in the wing play of the forwards; Athersmith and John Cowan have taken much longer than usual to get into form this season, but their fine runs in the Albion match showed us they were coming again, and at Derby a still further improvement was manifest, for both scored splendid goals, though Athersmith's effort was disallowed by a referee whose decisions have been more generally condemned than those of any man we can remember in the First League.

PROFESSIONAL REFEREES

● The whole question of refereeing needs overhauling badly. Personally, I can remember but two instances in many years where the faintest suspicion of partiality has attached to a referee, but while their fairness is unquestioned, the knowledge of the game possessed by many of the present officials seems to be less thorough than it should be in men wielding such powers. Most referees (in the League at least) would pass with honours an examination in the rules, but the keen sight, the freedom from excitement, and perfect nerve necessary to give an instant and just decision, are so rare, that the men combining all these qualities could be counted on one hand, and until the football authorities take a hint from their cricket brethren and appoint old professionals to this post, there is not much hope of any improvement.

WARM WELCOME

● The fickle public, though apt to neglect a man (and his house) when his day is supposed to be over, can be relied on to give him every encouragement when he tries his luck once more, a fact which was demonstrated at Small Heath on Saturday, when Hodgetts received a welcome such as has been accorded to no local footballer since that memorable day when Archie Hunter returned from his perhaps strategic visit to Scotland, to part no more in his playing days with the club which owed him so much. It is as yet too soon for his presence to work miracles with such an in-and-out team as Small Heath, who, from their present position in the table, seem destined to a term of probation in the lower division which will not be agreeable to their friends.

HANDSOME VICTORY

● The Aston Villa men have at last settled down to real business, and it will indeed be a great surprise if they fail to retain the League Championship trophy for another season. The team gave a splendid display at Derby last week, and thoroughly deserved their handsome victory. A large number of Villa supporters took advantage of the cheap excursions to witness the match, and had good value for the money, returning in much better spirits than was the case last January, when the County unexpectedly knocked the Birmingham club out of the English Cup competition.

THE CRITIC...

↪ *That fat linesman at Derby last Saturday fairly amused the crowd.*

↪ *Hodgetts was 'blowing' freely before all was over.*

and some steady back play by Methven that saved them from a much heavier defeat than they actually suffered. The Villa threw plenty of energy into their work, and their shooting was a great improvement on recent efforts. On one occasion Robinson four times within as many moments fisted and threw the ball out when a score seemed certain, but at length Campbell, with a pretty effort, put the Villa ahead. Athersmith next drove the ball into the net, but another mistake by the referee resulted in the goal being disallowed for off-side. Coming again, however, John Cowan scored a beauty from a fine centre by Athersmith, and the Villa won by 3 goals to 1.

Derby County: Robinson; Methven and A. Goodall; Cox, Turner and Kinsey; Goodchild, Bloomer, Miller, Stevenson and McQueen.

Aston Villa: Whitehouse; Spencer and Welford; Reynolds, James Cowan and Crabtree; Athersmith, Devey, Campbell, Wheldon and John Cowan.

● These teams met yesterday at Stoney Lane in the first round of the Staffordshire Cup competition, and as the result of a fast and exciting game the Albion won by 2 goals to 1.

The Villa were not fully represented, Welford, Reynolds, and Devey being absentees, whilst on the Albion side McLeod was not playing. During the first half the Villa, up-hill, did fairly well in midfield, and repeatedly troubled Reader, but generally speaking there was not much dash about them, and the Albion goalkeeper had no difficulty in stopping the shots sent in. On the other hand, the Albion, when they got away, were always dangerous, and as a result of some pretty runs they scored a couple of good goals. In the second half the Albion had much the best of the play until shortly before the close, when Crabtree changed places with Athersmith and went forward. The result was that Wheldon headed a pretty goal from a fine centre by Athersmith, but the Villa could not draw level, and the Albion fully deserved their victory.

The afternoon turned out fine, and there were about 5,000 specta-tors present. Albion won the toss, and played downhill. The first feature of interest was a free kick for the Albion, which Evans planted into the goal mouth. The ball was fouled and the Villa transferred the play to the top end. Williams was soon conspicuous and by a series of

Bob Chatt

throws-in on the left, Albion threat-ened danger, but they were penalised for tripping Wheldon. A combined effort was made by the Villa, Wheldon sending in a long shot, which Reader fisted out. A free kick for the Albion was well saved by Spencer, after which Garfield carried the ball into touch. A splendid effort by the Albion forwards ended in Richards shooting over the top. Darting away Athersmith made a fine run and shot well; Reader fum-bled, but a subsequent effort by Burton was cleared. The Villa were playing a vigorous game, and a fine cen-tre by John Cowan resulted in a corner, Banks fouled

CLEVER VILLA

● The Villa at present tie with Blackburn Rovers for third position in the League table. As they made such a mediocre commencement, they can scarcely be expected to get to the top before the end of November, but, once there, they ought to retain the position throughout the season, for the team is clever enough for anything.

HOPE FADES FOR HEATHENS

● When will Small Heath win another League match at home? They commenced the season excellently, and the manner in which they 'walked round' Newcastle United and Darwen inspired their supporters with confidence that they would regain their place in the First Division of the League. However, that hope has long since vanished, and the Heathens are at the present time much nearer the bottom of the list than their supporters relish. Seven points out of a possible sixteen is most unsatisfactory, and as they have allowed Lincoln City and Burton Swifts to defeat them on their own ground, besides having to be content with a draw against Gainsborough Trinity, it is not to be wondered at that their followers are growing discontented.

DENNIS 'RESTED'

● Those folks who expected Dennis Hodgetts to work miracles in the Small Heath team last week were sadly disappointed. He was rather slow and showed very little of his old form, which is not surprising considering that he has been 'resting' for more than six months. When he has settled down in his new home the ex-Villan will doubtless be of much service to the Second Leaguers; at present it is too early to judge of his capabilities.

OVER AND OUT

● Monday last saw the disappearance of our two principal Birmingham clubs from the Staffordshire Cup competition, Small Heath losing at Wolverhampton, while the Villa were unexpectedly defeated by the Albion at West Bromwich. The latter result is extremely disappointing to those who thought the Villa were going to carry everything before them.

26 OCTOBER 1896

HALESOWEN V ASTON VILLA RESERVES

● Considerable interest was manifested in this match, which was played on the Cricket Field, Halesowen, for notwithstanding the showery weather, the spectators numbered upwards of 2,000. The visitors won the toss, and the home team had to face the town end. Halesowen tried Swallow, the old Wolfrunian, in goal, and he received a hearty welcome from the spectators. Shortly after the commencement of hostilities Holden, one of the players, met with an accident, the ball striking him on the head, rendering him unconscious for a short time. The play throughout the game was very even, the goals being alternately attacked, both goalkeepers being kept well employed. Some excellent points were made by both sides, which were heartily recognised by the spectators, who during the progress of the game greatly increased in number, shortly before half-time the home team made a vigorous and united attack on the Villa's territory, and Edwards getting possession of the leather, and with the assistance of Sams succeeded in getting the first goal. On changing ends heavy rain occurred, which militated against the play. The Villa did most of the pressing, and but for Swallow being an excellent custodian must have scored. The home team afterwards got possession and severely pressed their opponents, eventually scoring. The Villa also by an excellent shot scored and the game ended in favour of Halesowen by 2 goals to 1.

close in goal, but Reader fisted out cleverly. The Albion went with a rush down the centre, but Spencer stopped them, and Parry subsequently shot outside. Williams twice saved when the Villa were dangerous, and Reader had to save from James Cowan. From a pass by Garfield, Ford raced away and shaved the post, and Williams shortly afterwards put the ball outside from a free kick. Athersmith and Chatt worked up the right, Reader having to save from the latter. Garfield again shot wide at the bottom end, but a minute later Ford scored a beauty. Restarting, Chatt got away, and compelled Reader to use his feet, whilst Evans stopped Wheldon just as he was about to shoot from close quarters. Ford was ruled offside when getting dangerous, and Wheldon touched the ball with his hand at the other end. The game continued fast and exciting, and Reader ran out 20 yards to clear, sending over the top of the stand. Garfield gave the Villa a corner, from which Reader cleverly saved, and Athersmith shot across goal and outside. Whitehouse saved at the other end, and Burton sent a long one over the top. The visitors continued to press. Athersmith and Campbell coming very near scoring. Reader made another clever save from Campbell, and the Albion backs both kicked among the crowd to clear. Spencer fouled the ball, and the free kick taken by Evans enabled Garfield to score a second for the Albion. Restarting, the Albion again went with a rush, Spencer and Evans having their work cut out to save. Going up the hill, Athersmith gave Campbell a chance, but he sent just outside. Reader saved a long shot by Wheldon, and Garfield was pulled up for off-side. Bassett sent in a fine long shot which Whitehouse cleared, and Athersmith forced a corner at the top, Reader cleverly saving the flag-kick. Garfield made another fine effort, but it came to nothing, and at half-time the score stood – Albion 2; Villa 0.

Crossing over the Albion forced a corner, which was followed by another, but both were cleared, and a subsequent centre by Bassett was very nearly put through by Garfield. Williams from a free kick sent over the top, and getting down the left Wheldon shot crossways over the top, when a touch to the centre might have scored. Flewitt got through the Villa backs and had a grand opening, but his final shot went just outside. Wheldon missed his mark at the other end, and from a free kick Crabtree saved. Wheldon got past the Albion backs, but Reader made a timely run-out and kicked into mid-field. The game was a characteristic Villa and Albion fight, but the Albion were much more dangerous than the Villa in their attacks for goal, Richards and Garfield made a splendid combined effort, and Ford landed one just over the top. Athersmith and Cowan both made clever efforts on their respective wings, and Flewitt made a fine effort. Reader had to handle from the centre of Athersmith, and Reader saved from Chatt and James Cowan. Breaking away, Flewitt shot well, while Garfield landed the leather outside. The Villa cleared a dangerous attack, and the Albion in turn had to act on the defensive. Athersmith centred well from the line, but the Villa were penalised for pushing, and subsequently Campbell sent wide. Crabtree (who had changed places with Chatt, and gone forward) sent in a long shot, and Reader took the ball away, apparently kicking Crabtree as he did so. The latter retaliated, and the referee had to come in as peace-maker. A free kick for the Villa was cleared, and Spencer from behind made a very erratic shot. Flewitt made a fine run and cross to Bassett, and the latter centred to Richards, who shot

CONTRACT AWARD

● The plans have been approved and the contract for the completion of the laying-out of the Villa's new home at the Lower Grounds. Mr W. Hopkins, builder, Thorp Street, has secured the contract, and with his experience at the Birmingham Racecourse, his name should be a guarantee for the quality and efficiency of the work. Mr E. B. Holmes, as architect, superintends the scheme.

GRUMBLERS, WHERE ARE YOU?

● Where are the grumblers to-day? A few weeks ago the local newspapers were inundated with letters from would-be critics who wished to advise the Aston Villa committee how to constitute their team in order that the League Championship Cup might be retained. Instead of taking any heed of these 'advisers,' the gentlemen who compose the Villa committee went their own sweet way, and that it is the right way is proved by the fact that the club at present occupy the third position in the League table, and are strong favourites for the Championship all over the country, although, of course, the chances of Preston North End, Bolton Wanderers, and Everton are not by any means to be despised.

DERBY DOUBLE SUCCESS

● To take four points from Derby County is certainly most meritorious, and the Villa players deserve all the good things which are being said of them. The team is not invincible; the days when a club could go through the League competition without suffering defeat have long since passed away, never to return again. Although the season is barely two months old, every club in both divisions of the League has suffered defeat upon at least one occasion. Sheffield United remained undefeated until last week, when they failed to survive a visit to Deepdale, the home of Preston North End.

FOR SALE – BUT NOT TO VILLA

● That the Aston Villa attack is exceedingly strong is proved by the fact that only two clubs in the League – Liverpool and Preston North End – have scored more goals this season than Birmingham's premier club. Still, the committee do not believe in missing the chance of booking a first-class player when one is in the market, and, consequently, when it was announced that Liverpool had decided to dispense with the services of Becton, the Villa were among the first with an offer for the transfer of his services. However, although a big sum was offered, Liverpool refused to deal, in consequence of a grudge which they owe the Villa, and they afterwards agreed to transfer Becton to Wolverhampton Wanderers for a consideration of £250. The player wishes to join the Villa, and absolutely refuses to sign for the Wolves; consequently, there is no idea whatever as to how the matter will end.

BRIEFLETS....

↪ *There is no truth in the statement published in a contemporary this week that Charlie Hare, the old Aston Villa forward, will shortly be seen in the ranks of Small Heath.*

↪ *A Sheffield paper on Monday stated that "Low refused £4 10s. from the Villa. He has signed for Glasgow Rangers for 25s. a week." We have to go away from home to learn the 'news.' Someone has obviously been 'spoofing' the Sheffield press.*

↪ *Small Heath are undoubtedly the 'surprise packet' of the season. When they are expected to lose, they win, and when they are deemed likely to have an easy task on hand, they either lose or draw. What can one make of their in-and-out form?*

into the net. The referee was allowing the point, but the linesman appealed, on the ground that the ball was out before Bassett centred, and the goal was then disallowed. Spencer sent in a fine shot, but the ball was fouled in goal. Both teams continued to work hard, but the Albion missed a couple of chances to add to their lead. The home defence was exceedingly good, Reader showing to great advantage. The half-backs were clever, and there was more dash among the forwards than usual. The Villa were not quite up to the mark, and although they played well in midfield they finessed too much in front of goal. Towards the close, however, Athersmith centred and Wheldon headed a fine goal. Result:- Albion, 2; Villa, 1.

West Bromwich Albion: Reader; Evans and Williams; Parry, Higgins and Banks; Bassett, Flewitt, Ford, Richards and Garfield.

Aston Villa: Whitehouse; Spencer and Evans; Burton, James Cowan and Crabtree; Athersmith, Chatt, Campbell, Wheldon and John Cowan.

Saturday 24th October 1896
VILLA 2, DERBY COUNTY 1

● Despite the unfavourable weather, and the counter-attraction of the Birmingham races, there was an attendance of nine or ten thousand present at Perry Barr, when the return match between the above clubs was played.

Both sides were fully representative, John Goodall and Leiper reappearing in their old places. The Villa won the toss and played down hill, having the advantage of a stiff breeze at their backs. They at once made tracks for the Derby goal. Devey being a moment too late to get in an effective shot, though he forced an unproductive corner. Derby got away on the right, but Archie Goodall shot over the bar, and then Devey and Athersmith made a dashing run, but shot wide. Campbell all but got through, and two more corners to the Villa were unproductive. Athersmith and Devey were in good form – the first-named particularly so – but John Cowan missed a fine centre, and Devey just shaved the posts. Robinson fisted out a warm attack, as he was bundled into the net, the operation being repeated a little later. A nice attack by Derby was spoiled by Stevenson getting offside, and when Wheldon got clean away he finished a grand run with a bad shot. Two fouls against the visitors were finely saved by Robinson, and the Derby goalkeeper several times cleared in marvellous fashion when a goal seemed inevitable. Another beautiful run and centre

by Athersmith was not utilised. Campbell, though almost under the bar, shooting over. John Cowan, too, had the goal open, but shot wide, and Devey followed suit, the Villa, although having all the best of the play, failing to get the ball through. Leiper, Methven, and Robinson had played splendidly for their side, and Turner amongst the halves was seen to great advantage.

John Cowan

The interval thus arrived with no goals scored.

In the second half, when playing against the wind, the Villa showed a much more formidable front, timing their passes better and shooting with more dash and precision. Campbell was the first to threaten danger, but he shot wide, and then Robinson effected another brilliant save from a fine shot of Cowan's; Bloomer and Goodall got off, but were quickly checked by Crabtree and Welford, and the Villa, going up again, Cowan completed a grand run and centre by Athersmith by heading into the net. At the other end Whitehouse cleverly stopped a warm shot by Miller, and Athersmith and Devey again getting off, Wheldon shot a second goal. Derby came with a rush and, Whitehouse misjudging a bouncing ball, Bloomer had no difficulty in breasting it through. Campbell and Wheldon missed good openings, and Stevenson, with

ALL ABOUT BECTON

● Should Liverpool take a sensible view of the case, and allow Becton to play for the club he desires to, the Villa can be regarded as exceedingly fortunate, for there are few cleverer players in the kingdom than Becton. He first came into prominence about five years ago with Preston North End, partnering John Cowan (now of Aston Villa) on the left wing. The season before last he had a disagreement with the Preston officials, and consequently the latter accepted an offer of £100 to transfer him to Liverpool. His displays with the Liverpool club have been consistently brilliant, and towards the close of the 1894-5 season he was selected to represent the English League against the Scottish League at Glasgow, in which contest his four comrades in the forward line were all Aston Villa men, viz., Athersmith (whom he partnered on the right wing,) Devey, Hodgetts, and Smith. Becton's form in this game so pleased the Villa officials present that they have since been very anxious to secure his services, and it is to be hoped that they will succeed in their endeavours.

FULL-BACK PRIORITY

● The Villa could certainly do with another first-class forward, but what they require more than anything at the present time is a champion back. Good players though Welford and Spencer undoubtedly are, they do not compare at all favourably with several other pairs in the League, Jones and Somerville, of Bolton Wanderers, for instance. Howard Spencer at one time appeared likely to develop into a champion, but he has not improved so greatly as his earlier form led one to expect, and it would be a good thing if a first-class man like Williams, Brandon, or Holmes to take his place. However, such men are not to be found at a moment's notice, and until the right man turns up it would be sheer folly to move Spencer from the team.

JAMES WELFORD

STEAMING TO STOKE

● Tomorrow (Saturday) the villa visit Stoke to play their return League match with the Pottery club, and will have to be in their very best form if they are to prove victorious. Last year the Villa were fortunate enough to obtain four points from the North Staffordshire club, and they may repeat the performance this season, although, as they only won at Perry Barr by the narrow margin of two goals to one, there is no ground for over-confidence. The L. and N. W. Railway Co. are running a cheap half-day excursion from Birmingham to Stoke to enable Villa supporters to witness the match, and as the team have been doing so well of late, there will doubtless be a large number of 'claret and blue' enthusiasts present.

BRIEFLETS....

☞ 'Surefoot' McKnight, the one-time Villan, is playing for Hurlford.

☞ Everton were promised £2 a man for beating the Villa at Perry Barr.

☞ According to the Scotch football agents, and English, too, Aston Villa are after about 9,704 juniors from across the border.

☞ An English official, a week or two ago, was told in Glasgow that unless he signed a youth up instantly, Aston Villa would in the evening. "Let 'em," he said, "they will lose him at Carlisle, and I can pick him up there."

THE CRITIC....

☞ Dorrell has not gained in pluck since he left Villa. He fairly funked it at Darwen.

☞ Now, Will Devey, not a goal in seven matches. This won't do, you know.

the goal open shot right into the hands of Whitehouse. Athersmith got clean through his opponents, and with no one to face but Robinson he shot wide. Nothing more was done, and the game, which finished amidst a terrific storm, ended in a win for the Villa by 2 goals to 1.

Derby County: Robinson; Methven and Leiper; Cox, A. Goodall and Turner; J. Goodall, Bloomer, Miller, Stevenson and McQueen.

Aston Villa: Whitehouse; Spencer and Welford; Reynolds, James Cowan and Crabtree; Athersmith, Devey, Campbell, Wheldon and John Cowan.

DIVISION ONE	P	W	L	D	F	A	Pt
Bolton Wanderers	9	6	1	2	15	5	14
Sheffield United	9	4	1	4	14	8	12
Aston Villa	9	5	2	2	15	12	12
Liverpool	11	5	4	2	19	12	12
Preston North End	8	4	1	3	18	13	11
Sheffield Wednesday	9	4	3	2	16	14	10
Blackburn Rovers	9	4	3	2	12	12	10
West Bromwich A.	9	3	3	3	8	10	9
Everton	8	4	4	0	12	14	8
Notts Forest	7	2	2	3	13	12	7
Burnley	9	2	4	3	14	19	7
Sunderland	10	2	5	3	10	18	7
Stoke	8	3	5	0	13	19	6
Derby County	8	2	5	1	15	17	5
Bury	8	1	4	3	5	13	5
Wolverhampton W.	9	2	6	1	10	12	5

LEAGUE DIVISION ONE

Saturday 31st October 1896
STOKE 0, VILLA 2

● There was a capital attendance at Stoke to witness the return League game between the home team and Aston Villa, a goodly contingent arriving in excellent time from Birmingham by the London and North Western excursion.

The Villa were without Crabtree and John Cowan, whose places were taken respectively by Burton and Smith. Stoke also were short of Eccles and Johnson. The Villa won the toss, but there was little wind to interfere with the play. After the opening exchanges, somewhat straggling in character, the Villa bore down on the right, and from a good shot by Athersmith, W. Rowley had to fist out, he repeating the operation a moment later from Devey. Brodie tripped Athersmith as he was getting ready to shoot, and from the foul, well placed by Reynolds, Wheldon steered the ball into the net six minutes from the start. The Villa were quickly attacking again, the forwards going down in a body, but Smith put the ball over the bar, and Devey shot wide. Stoke got up, and from a foul against Cowan Claire, with a long dropping shot, put the ball into the net, but as it had touched no one else no goal was scored. Stoke again attacked on the left, but Spencer cleverly stopped Schofield, and the Villa getting away Athersmith sent in a good centre, from which Wheldon hit the post, and Smith kicked over. W. Maxwell made a nice run and forced a corner, which was easily cleared, and Wheldon and Smith ran and dribbled past the Stoke backs, the former again hitting the post with a fine shot. A fruitless corner fell to the Villa, and Stoke broke away in the centre, a capital shot by Bouillemier dropping just over the bar. Wheldon made another splendid effort, but had hard luck, the ball rolling all along the goal line, and just outside. Whitehouse saved smartly from an attack on the left, and at the other end both Campbell and Athersmith sent in good ones, which were only a trifle short of the mark. Rowley was lucky in stopping a grand shot by Campbell, for he mulled the ball, but gathering it at the second attempt he succeeded in throwing behind. Nothing came of the corner, and when Wheldon again put the ball into the net he was given offside. A few minutes later Wheldon put in a beautiful overhead

VILLA SHOW CHAMPIONSHIP FORM

● Aston Villa are still the favourites for the League Championship, their excellent victory at Stoke last week enhancing their prospects considerably. Considering the fact that they were without the services of John Cowan and Crabtree, it was considered highly probable that the Birmingham club would have to be content with a draw, even if they were not defeated, for the Pottery club are a great team on their own ground, and, as one of their supporters enthusiastically remarked before the match, "they required a lot of beating." Well, they got what they required, without a doubt, for the Villa were in grand form, and thoroughly deserved their triumph.

LUCKY OCTOBER

● October has certainly been a lucky month for the Villa. They secured nine points out of a possible ten, three of the five League games which they have played having been away from home. No other club in the First Division has fared so well, and they have only to keep up their present form to be at the head of the table before another month is out.

SPENCER IN IRELAND

● Against Bury at Perry Barr tomorrow (Saturday) the Villa will not have their full strength, for Howard Spencer will be playing for the English League against the Irish League at Belfast. However, Crabtree and John Cowan will be back in the team again, and there is little doubt as to the result, although the abilities of Bury must certainly not be under-estimated. The Lancashire club have drawn their last three games, and as their team has been greatly improved since the commence-ment of the season, they can be relied upon to give spectators good value for their money. Mobley, the ex-Small Heath forward, was dropped last week, his place being taken by

HOWARD SPENCER

Pangbourne, the old Warwick County player, and so good was his display that it is doubtful if Mobley will regain his place in the team yet awhile.

BRIEFLETS

↪ *Becton, of Liverpool, is still idle. The Celtic club (Glasgow) made him a good offer last week, which he refused.*

↪ *Hereford Thistle are at present undefeated in the Birmingham League competition. Aston Villa Reserves pay them a visit tomorrow, and will have to be at their very best to win.*

↪ *The Villa Reserves have been giving anything but satisfaction this season; they have only scored 9 points out of nine matches in the Birmingham and District League.*

↪ *Aston Villa are making a big effort to get the English and Scotch International played at Aston Lower Grounds in April next.*

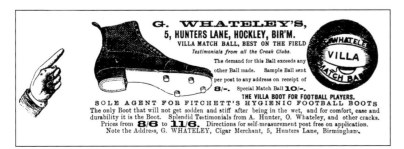
shot, but Rowley saved, and the interval arrived with the Villa leading by 1 goal to 0.

In the second half Stoke opened out more, and by their long kicks and rushing gave the Villa defence plenty to do. From a fine centre by Schofield, Eardley headed over the corner of the bar. From a free kick Stoke put the ball into the net, but again it had touched no one, and the point did not count. Two corners to Stoke were not further utilised, and then the Villa left and centre getting off, Wheldon shot into the net, the goal being disallowed for offside. Whiteside brought off a grand save from Eardley, the Villa at this point being unable to make any progress against the resolute play of their opponents. At length, however, a superb bout of passing by Athersmith, Devey, Wheldon, and Smith ended in the last-named shooting the second goal for the visitors, the ball going through Rowley's legs into the net. Exciting play followed to the close, but Stoke could make no impression on the visiting defence, the Villa winning by 2 goals to 0.

Stoke: W. Rowley; Clare and A. Rowley; Bouillemier, Sampson and Brodie; Eardley, A. Maxwell, Wood, W. Maxwell and Schofield.

Aston Villa: Whitehouse; Spencer and Welford; Reynolds, Cowan and Burton; Athersmith, Devey, Campbell, Wheldon and Smith.

LEAGUE DIVISION ONE
Saturday 7th November 1896
VILLA 1, BURY 1

● The weather in Birmingham was of a very disappointing character, rain falling heavily all the afternoon, and the consequence was that only a very moderate number of spectators assembled at Perry Barr to witness the game between Aston Villa and Bury.

The visitors were without Barbour and the Villa were minus Spencer and John Cowan. The Villa, playing up hill and against the wind and rain, at once forced the pace, but found Darroch in fine form, he frequently stopping the runs of both the home wings. The game, however, had not been long in progress when Athersmith got clear away, and with a long, dropping, curling shot he put the ball into the corner of the net – a very pretty though somewhat lucky goal. Bury came with a rush, and Evans missing his kick, Plant put in a goal shot which Whitehouse fisted out. The visitors came again, and Cowan put the ball back to the goalkeeper, who, hard pressed, managed to get it away in time. Some capital work by Crabtree was applauded, and then Campbell and Devey got off, the former passing neatly to Athersmith, who centred firmly, but only for Wheldon to put the ball out. Another nice run followed, but Wheldon's final effort was just over the bar. Even exchanges followed, each side pressing in turn, and then the Villa attacked strongly, Wheldon once more putting the ball over and Smith causing Montgomery to fist out. Athersmith put in a nice one, but the visiting custodian threw out to Reynolds, who returned the ball smartly, but Smith could not reach it in time to prevent it going behind. Bury played up hard, and for a time had the best of matters, and as the result of some capital work Millar made the score level with a capital shot well out of reach of Whitehouse. The Villa forced an unproductive corner, but nothing tangible was done up to the inter-val, when the teams crossed over with one goal each.

With the wind and rain behind them the Villa were expected to show up strongly, but they sadly disap-pointed their supporters. They stuck to the short-passing game, which, with a heavy, greasy ball and the wet, was easily combated by the strong kicking and dash of the visitors. Bury, indeed, played much better than in the first half, and though the Villa were always the cleverest they could make no impression on the other defence. They forced several corners, but none of them were utilised, whilst Bury frequently made dangerous incursions into the Villa half, and were always a source of trouble and anxiety to the home

RAIN DAMPENS EXPECTATIONS

● That Aston Villa are one of the strongest clubs in the kingdom at the present time no one will dispute for a moment, but it is impossible for even the best team in the world to win every match, and this fact should be remembered by those people who have been grumbling because the Villa failed to defeat Bury at Perry Barr last week. The weather was about as bad as it possibly could be, and it was really surprising to find that there were four thousand spectators present. The rain never ceased once during the whole ninety minutes the match was in progress, and the players had had enough of it long before the end came. Of course the result was a disappointment to the supporters of the League champions, a victory having been looked forward to as certain.

HORSES FOR COURSES

● The failure of the Villa to beat Bury at home need not be taken too much to heart by the club's supporters. They are likely to meet with few such miserable days in the rest of the present season, which is perhaps as well for their reputation, for luck enters largely into the game when the ball is so greasy that a player has little idea where it will go when he kicks it. The team, moreover, have always been noted as fair weather players, and it is like putting racehorses to ploughing to expect them to plunge about in the mud and slush which were so abundant at Perry Barr last Saturday. Indeed a suggestion has been made to the committee by some facetious enthusiast that they should run two teams, one for the delicate finessing suitable for dry ground, the other for mudlarking, but even the resources of the Villa could not bear that strain.

WELL DONE, WELFORD

● Welford was the only man in the team who really shone, the halfbacks and forwards (with the exception of Athersmith) being a poor lot, their stamina proving insufficient for the work they were called upon to do, and the inexcusable mistake was made of neglecting Athersmith, the one player in the team who is indifferent to the weather. However, after the comments of their best friends the men may be trusted not to repeat that blunder, for a week or two at least.

ROOM FOR BECTON?

● Another item which should have the effect of sharpening the wits of some of the forwards, is the announcement that the Villa Committee have repeated their offer of £250 for Becton; if they get him, and they undoubtedly will if that player does not change his mind, room will have to be found for him, for that price would not be paid for a reserve man, and it is no secret who would be asked to stand down for him.

SMITH RETURNS

● Howard Spencer being away at Belfast, Evans gained a place in the first team, and played an excellent game at right back, fully justifying all the good things that have been said concerning him. Steve Smith, the other reserve player in the team, also did well, though it is to be feared that we shall never see him in such form as he exhibited a couple of seasons ago, when he proved himself to be the best outside left forward in the country. His injury at Bramall Lane last year appears to have taken a lot of the pluck out of him, which is perhaps not to be wondered at.

BRIEFLET...

☞ *Peter Boyle, the player who was reported to have joined the Aston Villa last week, has thrown in his lot with Sunderland. Some of the local papers were rather premature in announcing his capture.*

players. Athersmith and Devey both missed good openings, whilst on the other side Pangborne and Plant made capital efforts, and Wylie, with a long shot, caused Whitehouse to throw out. Try as they would the Villa could not get in front, Darroch in particular distinguishing himself by his brilliant defence. Nothing more was scored, and the game ended in a draw of 1 goal each.

Bury: Montgomery; Darroch and Davidson; Pray, Clegg, and Ross; Wyllie, Pangborne, Millar, Henderson and Plant.

Aston Villa: Whitehouse; Evans and Welford; Reynolds, Cowan, and Crabtree; Athersmith, Devey, Campbell, Wheldon and Smith.

● Sheffield Wednesday are not going so strongly just now, and though Aston Villa were the visiting team on Saturday there was nothing like the usual attendance at Olive Grove.

Both sides were well represented, though the Villa were still without John Cowan and had to substitute Chatt for Reynolds, the latter being indisposed. There was a cross wind blowing, and the Villa winning the toss took what little advantage there was to be obtained from it. They at once got down to the other end, and from a foul the ball was so nicely placed that Wheldon headed into the net a couple of minutes from the start. They looked like scoring again almost immediately, but Langley upset Athersmith and Massey cleared. The latter and Earp were once more in the way when the visiting left looked dangerous, and then the game became rather rough, fouls being frequent, though the referee interfered far too often and when there was not the slightest reason. From a free kick Davis put in a fine shot, but Whitehouse saved at the expense of an unproductive corner. Sheffield came again, and from a nice centre by Bell, Davis had the goal open, but put the ball yards over the bar, Spikesley following suit a little later. From another foul Devey was very unlucky in not scoring, and Smith, after making a grand run, shot wide. The Wednesday played up hard, and did some good work on the wings,  *Johnny Campbell* especially Bell, Brady, and Spikesley, but their final efforts were very moderate, and with Spencer and Welford − especially the latter − in form, their attacks came to nothing. The Sheffield goal next had a very lucky escape from Devey, and after Smith had hit the side of the net Wheldon, with a grand shot, dropped the ball on the bar. Nothing more was done, and the Villa crossed over leading by a goal to nothing. For the first quarter of an hour of the second half the home team had all the best of the play, and made the pace very hot. Fortunately, however, the Villa defence was sound. Welford doing some magnificent work, but at length Brady equalised with a beautifully-got goal. This stimulated the Villa to renewed efforts, and they set about their opponents in fine style. Campbell made a splendid run, aided by Wheldon, and finished up a brilliant effort with a screw shot which put the ball into the corner of the net, whilst a few moments later Athersmith headed a third goal, after Devey had forced Massey to clear. Thenceforward the Villa had the best of the play to the finish, and won handsomely by 3 goals to 1.

Sheffield Wednesday: Massey; Earp and Langley; Brandon, Crawshaw and Jamieson; Bell, Brash, Davis, Brady and Spikesley.

Aston Villa: Whitehouse; Spencer and Welford; Chatt, Cowan and Crabtree; Athersmith, Devey, Campbell, Wheldon and Smith.

TOP BILL AT THE OLIVE GROVE

● English Cupholders v League Champions! This is the bill of fare for tomorrow, and as the game is to be played at Olive Grove there will no doubt be a very interesting contest. Sheffield Wednesday commenced the season in very poor style, but, to quote George Beauchamp, "they're coming on again," and at the present time they are going great guns, but if the Villa give as good an exhibition as they have in their other out matches they ought to pull through all right. Last season they took four points from the Wednesday, winning at Perry Barr by two goals to one and at Olive Grove by three goals to one, in addition to defeating them in the Birmingham Cup competition by four goals to three at Olive Grove.

HARE TURNS HEATHEN

● There have been a good many rumours about the old Warwick County-cum-Aston Villa-cum-Woolwich Arsenal forward, Charlie Hare, lately, but Hare has at last been transferred to the Coventry Road club, who are to be congratulated upon their smart capture.

BRIEFLETS...

↪ *Those football enthusiasts who desire to possess a photo of the League Championship Cup, at present held by the Villa, should call at Thompson's photographers, Lozells Road (near Six Ways) Aston, where they are to be purchased.*

↪ *Hereford Thistle had won all their Birmingham League matches up to Saturday last, when they were defeated at home by Aston Villa Reserves.*

AWKWARD QUESTIONS

● Will Aston Villa win the League Championship this season?
● How did their supporters relish the inability of the team to defeat Bury on Saturday?
● How would those critics who disparaged the Villa's display care to be in the drenching rain for ninety minutes?
● Why was the back row of the press-box at Perry Barr filled, while the front row was unoccupied?
● Did the critics prefer watching the game through misty windows, or were they afraid of the rain?
● What pleasure could ladies possibly have in watching a game of football on such a miserable afternoon?
● Would they not have been better employed at home darning socks or assisting in the housework rather than catching colds at Perry Barr?
● Is Jack Devey the best captain the Villa could have?
● Would not Crabtree be a better man for the post?
● Will Charlie Hare play for Small Heath against his old comrades tomorrow?
● Will Charlie Athersmith care to visit Bury when the Villa play their return match with the Lancastrians?
● Will he not be cautious, after the way he treated Ross (when the referee was not looking) on Saturday?

THE CRITIC...

↪ *Don't descend to such cowardly tricks, Athersmith!*

↪ *The Villa men are badly in need of a stimulant – before a match begins.*

↪ *The Villa lay all the blame on the rain. Rot!*

↪ *Two prominent Birmingham critics swore dreadfully in the Perry Barr press-box on Saturday at the ineptitude of the Villa. No wonder!*

↪ *Wheldon seemed afraid to hurt the ball.*

Saturday 21st November 1896
VILLA 4, SHEFFIELD WED. 0

● The weather being fine, there was an attendance of about 14,000 spectators at Perry Barr to witness the return match between the Villa and Sheffield Wednesday. The home side was the same as at Sheffield the week previous, whilst Wednesday substituted Ferrier for Brady, Bell going centre and Davis partnering Spikesley.

The Villa won the toss and played down hill, there being little advantage in the cross wind. The home team at once began to force the pace. Wheldon forcing Massey to handle, and then putting the ball just over the bar. The Sheffield right got away and centred across to Spikesley, who spoiled a good piece of play by a bad shot. Each side tried hard and attacked in turn, and though the Villa had considerably the best of the play they had no luck with their shots, which went anywhere but into the net. From a grand run and centre by Athersmith, Wheldon headed right into goal. Massey being extremely lucky to turn it on one side as the ball was going into the net. Nothing came from the corner, but the Villa continued the pressure, Campbell and Athersmith missing by the narrowest of shaves. On the other side Bell and Davis, the latter especially, were frequently dangerous, but they found the home defence too sound and seldom got in a serious shot. Spikesley was too well watched by Chatt to cause much trouble. Wheldon hit the bar with a grand shot, and a foul under the posts was cleared, nothing having been scored up to the interval.

On resuming, the Villa at once made it evident that they meant business. Their combination was grand, and they played with exceptional dash and resolution. Within a few minutes of the restart, Smith made a fine run, and though temporarily stopped by Earp, he came again and with a lovely screw shot put the ball into the net. Then Cowan sent in a beauty which

Steve Smith

Massey was lucky to tip over the bar, a similar fate that attended a splendid effort by Wheldon. Hands against Spencer gave Sheffield a beautiful opening, but the ball was got away, and a dashing piece of play by Campbell and Athersmith resulted in the latter scoring the second goal. Ferrier came away nicely and hit the bar, but the Villa were soon off again, a brilliant run and centre by Smith ending in Devey running the ball into the net. Smith again ran in magnificent style, but his final shot was weak, and when Bell got in a good one Whitehouse saved in clever fashion. A fast sprint and accurate centre by Athersmith was met by Wheldon who headed past Massey, and a fast and interesting game thus ended in favour of the Villa by 4 goals to 0.

Sheffield Wednesday: Massey; Earp and Langley; Brandon, Crawshaw and Jamieson; Brash, Ferrier, Bell, Davis and Spikesley.

Aston Villa: Whitehouse; Spencer and Welford; Chatt, James Cowan and Crabtree; Athersmith, Devey, Campbell, Wheldon and Smith.

CARD CRITICISM

● The 'official card and bulletin' of the Aston Villa Football Club is a wonderful affair, and is guaranteed to deceive the cutest of those who speculate a penny on it. I have visited Perry Barr some half-dozen times this season to see the Villa perform, and on each occasion have discovered some errors in their 'official card.' For instance, in the Everton match, Cameron was supposed to be playing centre-forward for the visitors, whereas in reality Hartley occupied that position, while on Saturday last, although Barbour's name appeared on the card as playing at back for Bury, that player did not even come to Birmingham. Of course the Villa committee cannot foresee these errors; the names of the teams, as selected, are given to the printers, and they concern themselves no more about the matter. However, at West Bromwich – despised West Bromwich – affairs are managed very differently: when changes are made in either team the spectators are notified by means of a blackboard carried round the field announcing what alterations have been made from the names printed on the card. The Villa might well follow the example of their Black Country rivals.

Another glaring error on the 'official card and bulletin' of Saturday last was, that, although the Villa were thrown out of the Staffordshire Cup competition several weeks ago, they have still special dates set apart for the third round, the semi final, and even the final. How the Albion folks would smile when they saw it!

20 NOVEMBER 1896

PETS ARE POISED

● The football season is not yet three months old, and many surprises may occur between now and the end of next April, but there is at present every indication that Aston Villa will retain possession of the League Championship Cup for another year. Bolton Wanderers are at the head of the League as yet, but the Villa are close behind, having played, won, lost, and drawn the same number of matches as the 'Trotters,' but possessing a slightly inferior goal average. Should the Villa defeat Sheffield Wednesday at Perry Barr to-morrow and Bolton succumb at Preston – both very likely occurrences – the Perry Pets will be at the top of the Championship table once again, and should be able to hold the position against all comers.

BEST AWAY

● It cannot be denied that the performances of the Villa away from home have been of a much more brilliant character than their exhibitions at Perry Barr so far this season. They have gained eight points out of a possible twelve at home, while on foreign soil they have captured nine out of a possible twelve. Yet some folks consider the display of the team is very unsatisfactory!

CHATT GIVES SATISFACTION...

● Sheffield Wednesday were unable to prevent the Villa from adding two points to their score on Saturday, for, although the 'Blades' were in fine trim, the Birmingham team played in their best form, and secured a thoroughly well-deserved victory by three goals to one. At the last moment Reynolds was taken ill, and Chatt was called upon to take his place, the display of the ex-Ironopolis man giving entire satisfaction to all – except Spikesley and his partner. John Cowan was still an absentee, although his leg is almost right again, but the Committee are acting very wisely in 'resting' him as long as they have such a capable player as Steve Smith to fall back upon.

...AND SO DOES SMITH

● Not the least satisfactory feature about the Villa's handsome win at Sheffield is the remarkable improvement shown by Steve Smith. His play

---

Saturday 28th November 1896

BLACKBURN ROVERS 1, VILLA 5

● There was only a moderate crowd at Ewood Park on Saturday to witness the game between Blackburn Rovers and Aston Villa. One or two changes were made in the home team, and the Villa had to play Evans in place of Welford at full back, the latter having injured his ankle.

The Rovers won the toss, and the Villa kicked off against a cross wind, Wheldon, with a long shot, just missing. Each side attacked in turn, but the play for a time was of shambling order. An unproductive corner fell to the Rovers, and then Whitehead was left with a nice opening, but shot high over the bar. Whitehead missed another chance soon after, and then Wheldon and Devey tried goal shots, which were cleverly saved by Joy. Indeed, the latter greatly distinguished himself during the first half hour, though eventually a very fine screw shot from Devey headed into the corner of the net out of his reach. Some interesting exchanges followed, though the Villa were clearly not over-exerting themselves, and the interval arrived with the Villa leading by 1 goal to 0.

In the second half Houlker and Killean changed places, but though this had the effect of improving the Rovers' attack, the result speedily became a foregone conclusion. It was only very occasionally that the Rovers broke away, but they found one or two openings that ought certainly to have been improved on had there been the least steadiness in their attack. Chippendale being a conspicuous defaulter. The Villa, on the other hand, settled down to serious business, and kept the home defence constantly at work. After a fine run and centre by Athersmith, Devey shot hard into goal, Joy caught the ball, but was not quick enough in getting it away, with the result that Wheldon came up and put it into the net. Still pressing, the Villa continued to make things warm, and Cowan sent in a terrific shot, which Joy fumbled, and, before he could recover himself, Smith was in attendance and kicked the ball through. The Rovers wakened up after this, and, from a foul in a good position, the ball was put into the Villa goal, having just touched Whitehouse in its flight. The Villa were once again put on the mettle, and, from a beautiful run and centre by Athersmith, Wheldon headed into the net; whilst just before the close the latter scored again with a rasping shot from quite 30 yards' range. The Villa thus won in handsome style by 5 goals to 1.

Blackburn Rovers: Joy; Brandon and Anderson; Booth, Dewer and Houlker; Wilmington, Whitehead, Killean, Chippendale and Campbell.

Aston Villa: Whitehouse; Spencer and Evans; Chatt, Cowan and Crabtree; Athersmith, Devey, Campbell, Wheldon and Smiths.

DIVISION ONE	P	W	L	D	F	A	Pt
Aston Villa	14	9	2	3	31	15	21
Bolton Wanderers	13	8	2	3	23	12	19
Liverpool	16	7	5	4	23	15	18
Preston North End	14	7	3	4	32	21	18
Sheffield United	12	5	1	6	19	12	16
Derby County	14	6	6	2	34	25	14
West Brom	14	5	5	4	12	14	14
Notts Forest	13	4	5	5	22	20	13
Sheffield Wednesday	13	5	5	3	21	24	13
Blackburn Rovers	14	5	6	3	14	27	13
Everton	12	5	5	2	20	17	12
Bury	13	3	4	6	17	22	12
Stoke	14	4	9	1	21	36	9
Wolverhampton W.	12	3	7	2	14	15	8
Burnley	13	2	8	3	16	31	7
Sunderland	13	2	8	3	11	24	7

---

with the reserves certainly did not prepare us for the clever exhibitions he has given since John Cowan's accident called him once more to the first team, he being only slow, but apparently tender on his legs, and it has been repeatedly remarked in the stand that he would never again be worth his place in the League team. But whether it is the extra training the first team receive, or whether he was reserving his energies, the fact remains that he has been quite a different man since he has been seriously asked to justify his position as a football player. His display against Bury raised hopes in the Villa supporters that

STEVE SMITH

he would yet be able to repeat those electrifying runs against which no defence availed, and which have so often bewildered Hugh Wilson when that finest of half-backs was at his best; and at Sheffield a still further improvement was noticed, the left wing being considered even stronger than the right, though it is only fair to Athersmith to say that this was not his fault.

BRIEFLETS...

☞ *Aston Villa pay a visit to Stoke on Monday week, the 30th inst., to play a friendly match with the 'Potters' for Billy Dickson's benefit.*

☞ *Gray, who a couple of seasons ago was with Aston Villa Reserves, is at present playing with Grimsby Town.*

27 NOVEMBER 1896

CAMPBELL THE CHARMER

● There was a time when to see the Villa score four goals at Perry Barr would not have driven their supporters wild with delight, but goals nowadays don't come so easily as they once did: there is more attention paid to the defence, and goal-keepers are, as a class far superior to what they were. Two is the most the Villa had scored in a League match at home up to Saturday, and when half time arrived without one, most people would have sold their chance for a single point, but after the interval it was noticed that the front line had adopted a new formation, the inside wing men falling back a little, leaving Campbell to do the rushing while they were ready to tackle the defenders who should chance to rob him, and it worked like a charm. Campbell has never before given a show at Perry Barr within streets of his display on Saturday, and the committee would not change him for any centre-forward now playing.

SMITH TO STAY?

● Steve Smith is playing so well for the Villa at the present time that it would be unwise for the Committee to move him, even if John Cowan has completely recovered. The old Hednesford player has a liking for the Ewood Park enclosure, as, two seasons ago, he scored five goals there, viz., when the Villa defeated the Rovers in a League match (2-0,) and, later in the season, when they beat Sunderland in the semi-final for the English Cup (3-1) on that ground. He ought certainly to play there tomorrow.

DEAR, OH DEAR!

● What is the matter with Aston Villa Reserves? For a team that includes such renowned players as Wilkes, Reynolds, Burton, and Evans it is a positive disgrace to be defeated by Small Heath Reserves by three goals to nothing, and many people are wondering why Jimmy Elliott, who is a first-class back, and is at present receiving good wages from the Villa club, is allowed to remain idle. If his services are not required for either the first or second team, why is he not put on the transfer list? There are plenty of Second Division League clubs who would be glad to get hold of him.

● This match, for the benefit of William Dickson, formerly centre forward for Aston Villa, but who has been with the Stoke Club for some five years, was played yesterday afternoon on the Stoke ground. Dickson has become deservedly popular amongst his Pottery friends, as he has shown persistently steady endeavour to uphold the honour of the Stoke Club. He was injured some time ago in the match against Sheffield Wednesday, and, although not yet able to play for Stoke, is recovering from his injury.

The weather was beautifully fine, but bitterly cold, and the ground was very hard, as the result of the sharp frost. There would be about 2,000 persons present when the ball was kicked off at three o'clock, but we understand that a large number of tickets had been disposed of, so that the financial result to Dickson will in all probability be a very satisfactory one.

Billy Dickson

Campbell kicked off for the Villa, and after the opening exchanges the Pottery team pressed, and looked dangerous on more than one occasion, but did not score. At length they secured a corner, from which Bentley scored the first goal for Stoke with a shot which Wilkes could not possibly get. This was after more than a quarter of an hour's play, and almost immediately after the ball had been restarted Allan Maxwell put in a beautiful shot, which Wilkes cleverly saved. The Villa left wing next pressed, and although this was for the moment relieved the right wing went down, and Campbell in the centre put in a pretty shot, which Johnson cleverly saved. The Villa centre again showed brilliant form, and Johnson, running out, kicked away in the nick of time, a performance loudly cheered by the spectators. Wilkes next had to kick away. A pretty piece of combined play by Schofield and Willie Maxwell appeared to put the Aston goal at the mercy of Bentley, to whom the ball was passed, but the latter kicked over. Spencer then relieved a renewed attack, and the ball was quickly transferred to the Stoke territory, where Durber proved equal to the emergency. Campbell again caused Johnson to run out and kick away. The Villans were pressing, but the Pottery defence was praiseworthily sound. Cowan next put in a swift shot, which only just missed its mark. Stoke next assumed the aggressive, and Wilkes had to stop the ball twice, one being a capital low shot by Schofield. Again the homesters maintained a good attack, but Schofield missed the goal. Spencer next distinguished himself by a particularly clever bit of play. After a time Schofield put in a great shot, which Wilkes saved grandly. Nothing more came before half-time, the score being – Stoke, 1; Aston Villa, 0.

The game had not been resumed more than half-a-minute when, from a centre by Eardley, Willie Maxwell scored for the homesters. Wilkes had to handle directly afterwards, and saved very cleverly again from Allan Maxwell. Eardley shot wide, and Schofield, after a fast, run, over. Johnson fisted out a shot by Devey. Wilkes saved from Allan Maxwell, conceding a corner, from which nothing came, and then Johnson had to throw away after fine play by Wheldon. Eardley scored a third goal with a low shot three minutes from the completion of play. The match concluded in a victory for Stoke by 3 goals to 0.

Stoke: Johnson; Clare and Durber; Brodie, Grower and Rowley; Eardley, Bentley, A. Maxwell, W. S. Maxwell and Schofield. .

Aston Villa: Wilkes; Spencer and Evans; Reynolds, James Cowan and Crabtree; Athersmith, Devey, Campbell, Harvey and Wheldon.

DESERVING DICKSON

● Aston Villa go to Stoke today to play a benefit match for W. Dickson. There is no more honest, straightforward, and deserving football player living than our genial friend 'Billy' Dickson, and I trust he will receive the bumping gate he deserves. For three years he was associated with the Villa Club, and as centre forward led them to many a victory. Afterwards he was transferred by mutual consent to Stoke, and I have it on the testimony of the secretary – the famous goalkeeper, W. Rowley – that no man has done more than Dickson to improve the tone and quality of the Pottery team. Then, here's good luck to him!

4 DECEMBER 1896

REYNOLDS RUMOUR

● The person who started the rumour that Reynolds, the famous Aston Villa half back, had been guilty of misconduct, and was consequently in the 'black books' of the committee, has been very careful to keep his identity a secret, or he might find himself the defendant in an action for slander. Stories that are at all to the discredit of a player are soon circulated among footballers, and it is a good thing that the Villa committee considered the matter worth the trouble of contradictions, for if they had not done so the story would have spread – and grown considerably in the spreading – until we should have been told that he had been drunk for several weeks past, that he had threatened to murder the other innocent young players, and that the committee had suspended him indefinitely. As it is, we learn that Reynolds is behaving himself as well as anyone could wish, and the only matter for regret is that the people who have repeated the slanders concerning him cannot be found so that he could take a few 'penalty kicks' at them.

AWKWARD QUESTIONS

● What has become of the *Argus's* anonymous football correspondents of late? Are 'Villa Supporter,' 'Villa Member,' 'Bellows to Mend,' and the other nonsensical scribes asleep, or have they seen the folly of their ways?

BECTON STAYS AT LIVERPOOL

● So the much-talked-of Becton is to remain at Liverpool, after all! The news that his old club had decided to retain his services came as a bitter disappointment to Aston Villa supporters, who had confidently anticipated seeing him donning the colours of the League Champions before Christmas arrived. Becton is disappointed almost as much as the Villa committee are at the decision of the Liverpool club, for he had set his heart upon coming to Birmingham. Had he done so, it is reckoned that he would have cost the Villa club something like £10 per week for the rest of the season, this amount of course, including the money which they would have paid for his transfer. Still, he would probably have been worth even that enormous sum. for there are few better forwards than he in the kingdom at the present time. However, it is of little use talking of what might have been: Becton remains at Liverpool, and the matter is at an end.

ATHERSMITH ON VIEW

● Having no League match to play tomorrow, Aston Villa visit the Metropolis to meet that famous band of amateurs, the Corinthians. Matches between these two teams are always interesting, probably because the Villa play in a rather different style to other clubs in 'friendlies': they know that they are being watched by critical eyes, and as most of the

● Having no League engagement on Saturday, Aston Villa played a friendly match against the Corinthians at the Queen's Club, West Kensington. There was not a very large attendance. The amateurs were thoroughly representative, whilst the Villa had Whitehouse and Welford away.

The Corinthians played with the wind and sun at their backs, and had all the best of the opening exchanges until the Villa left, breaking away in good style, Wheldon scored with a grand shot, which curled in just under the bar. The amateurs speedily attacked again, Gettings, Gosling and Collier being prominent, but the last named's shot was well saved by Wilkes at the expense of an unproductive corner. Lodge cleared from Athersmith, and Campbell and Devey shot over the bar. The amateurs were frequently dangerous from strong rushes, but their efforts were too wayward in character to be effective, and the Villa going up forced a corner. The ball was got away, but Evans dropped it back, and Harrison had not time to clear before Devey jumped up and headed into the net. Directly afterwards a miskick by Evans let in the amateur right, and Collier scored with a fine ground shot, but this only served to stimulate the Villa, and a few moments later, from a beautiful centre by Athersmith, Wheldon headed another goal. Lively play followed but nothing more was done up to the interval, when the Villa led by 3 goals to 1.

On resuming the home side were the first to attack, and Evans tripping Alexander within the 12 yards limit, a penalty kick was given against him, from which the latter had no difficulty in scoring. The Villa gained a corner, but though the ball was well placed nothing came of it; though directly after-wards they came again, and

Albert Evans

Campbell put on the fourth goal. Wheldon, Athersmith, and Campbell all made goal shots, but though Harrison twice almost let the ball go through, he managed to save. The Villa defence were kept busy, having plenty to do to stop the powerful rushes of the amateurs. Bursup, Collier, Gettings, and Reynolds all being conspicuous for good work. Collier put on the third point, and about three minutes to time Alexander equalised with a grand low shot, an interesting game ending in a draw of 4 goals each.

Corinthians: Harrison; Lodge and Oakley; Foster, Reynolds and Middleditch; Gosling, Collier, Gettings, Alexander and Bursup.

Aston Villa: Wilkes; Spencer and Evans; Chatt, Cowan and Crabtree; Athersmith, Devey, Campbell, Wheldon and Smith.

● This match, for the benefit of the widow and children of the late Joe Powell, of the Arsenal Club, attracted 6,000 people to Plumstead.

The game was a fast and good one, and nothing was scored for half-an-hour, when Wheldon, Cowan, and Devey scored goals in quick succession for the Villa, who were leading at half-time by 3 to 0.

In the second half Harwood scored for the Arsenal, who had a lot of the game. However, neither side scored again, and an interesting match resulted:- Villa, 3 goals; Woolwich, 1.

gentlemen who select the international elevens to do duty for England are present, it behoves them to be at their best. Should Athersmith play in anything like his usual form in this game, Bassett will probably have cause to grieve when next March comes around. It may be so. Who knows?

RELAXING IN LONDON

● As the team has no League engagement this week, the men have been let off their usual training, a compliment to Mr. Jackson's eleven (whom they play tomorrow, Saturday) he will be far from appreciating, but though the men like to shine in London the committee are wise in relaxing the bow a little: it ought to come back with all the more spring.

7 DECEMBER 1896

POWELL BENEFIT

● Owing to the Villa, with their usual kindliness, having volunteered to play a match against Woolwich Arsenal at Plumstead today for the benefit of the widow of the Arsenal back, Powell, who died from blood-poisoning last week, the smoking concert and presentation to John Devey at the Old Royal Hotel is postponed until next Monday evening. The Villa players go to Plumstead for 'bare expenses' only, all the men giving their services.

ELLIOTT BENEFIT

● Jimmy Elliott, who came from Middlesbrough Ironopolis to the Villa four years ago, is to have a benefit on Tuesday, the 28th Inst., when Small Heath will oppose the League champions at Perry Barr. Elliott's health has been far from good of late, and it is probable that he has made his last appearance in first-class football. he was always a tryer, and one of the pluckiest men I have known for his inches. I hope he will get a bumper.

11 DECEMBER 1896

SCORELINE A TRUE REFLECTION

● Although friendly matches in the Midlands are regarded as 'played out,' there are still many people in the South of England who consider such games worth witnessing, as was evidenced on Saturday last at the Queen's Club ground, Kensington, when, although the lowest admission fee was a shilling, there were over four thousand spectators at the Corinthians v Aston Villa match. The amateurs were very anxious to defeat the League Champions, and showed their very best form throughout, but, despite the fact that the Villa players did not exert themselves so much as they would in a League game, the Londoners could only succeed in making a draw, the score of four goals each being a true reflex of the play.

BLACKBURN WANT 'BALDY'

● Blackburn Rovers are badly in want of new players, and are making strenuous efforts to strengthen their team. Haydock has already been induced to return to them, and played for them last week, while Nicol, the well-known Burnley footballer, has just been transferred to them. An emissary from the Rovers was in Birmingham last week to persuade, if possible, the Villa to transfer Reynolds to them, but the League Champions do not intend to part with 'the veteran' yet awhile: he will be very useful should one of the regular halves get injured or go 'off colour.' Though his appearance betokens age, Reynolds is by no means the oldest player belonging to the Villa club, and he has plenty of good football in him yet.

CHARITABLE CAUSE

● The generous action of the Aston Villa club in playing a friendly match

Saturday 12th December 1896
BURNLEY 1, VILLA 2

● The Villa had a fruitless journey to Turf Moor on Saturday to play their first League match with Burnley. The weather was terribly wet, and the ground covered with pools of water. A start was made, though the ground was certainly not fit for League football, and, after the game had lasted a little over half-an-hour, the referee stopped the game, and the match will have to be played again.

Both clubs were well represented. The Villa had Welford back in his old place, but Campbell was away with a severe cold, and Crabtree going up to centre forward. Reynolds came into the team again as left half-back. Burnley played two of their latest acquisitions, Longair and Hartley, of Sunderland, the former a centre-half and the latter left inside forward. So far as the game went the Villa were much the cleverer team, but accurate kicking or passing was totally out of the question. After playing about 25 minutes Reynolds was penalised for a foul throw-in, and Place, sen., putting the ball in nicely, Hill shot hard against the inside of the bar, and from the rebound Hartley met the ball and steered it safely into the net. The Villa at once went down the field – having the wind and rain at their backs – and from a scrimmage Athersmith equalised, whilst a moment later Crabtree scored again with a beautiful oblique shot. Mr. Armitt, the referee, then consulted with the linesmen, and they decided to declare the match off, the Villa at this point leading by 2 goals to 1.

Burnley: Haddow; Reynolds and McLintock; Place (sen), Longair, and Taylor; Beveridge, Hill, Bowes, Hartley, and Place (jun).

Aston Villa: Whitehouse; Spencer and Welford; Chatt, Cowan and Reynolds; Athersmith, Devey, Crabtree, Wheldon and Smith.

Monday 14th December 1896
BERWICK RANGERS 1, VILLA 5

● The fortunes of the draw brought Berwick Rangers first out of the hat against the Villa, and the League Champions had to journey to Worcester yesterday to play their Birmingham Cup-tie. Unfortunately the weather was cold and wet, or the visit of the Villa first eleven would have been a great attraction at Worcester. As it was, about a couple of thousand spectators were present, and though the home team were of course outclassed, they greatly enjoyed the football shown by the visitors.

The Villa took matters pretty easily, and won by 5 goals to 1, though, but for the excellent goal-keeping of Benwell, the score would have been much heavier. The Rangers kicked-off, but the Villa were soon down, only, however, to drive the ball over. They soon came again, and from pretty play by Wheldon the ball was sent across to Athersmith, who centred finely, but

Bob Chatt

Crabtree's final shot was over the bar. Some nice play by the Rangers put their left on the attack, but Spencer stopped them cleverly, and the visitors going up again, Wheldon tried a long one, which went over the bar. Wigley made a grand run down the left and centred cleverly, but Higgins did not utilise the opening, and Welford cleared easily. The Villa were attacking strongly when Wheldon was given offside, but a foul for 'hands' put them in possession again, and Wheldon hit the side of the net. The Rangers were going strongly, and a pretty piece of work by Higgins gave Wigley a chance, but Welford rushed across and got the ball with Woolwich Arsenal on Monday last, for the benefit of the family of the late Joe Powell, the Arsenal back, has been warmly commended in all quarters. No club in the kingdom has done more in the cause of charity, and Birmingham people have every reason to be highly proud of their club.

SPECIALIST CARE

● Griffiths and John Cowan, both of Aston Villa, have been under the care of Dr. Walter Whitehead, the famous Manchester bone specialist, and are progressing as favourably as could be desired. With Steve Smith playing so brilliantly at the present time, however, it is doubtful if John Cowan will regain his position in the first team when he has quite recovered.

SMALL HEATH'S 'BEST' RESULT

● No matter whether the Small Heath players are taking part in a League game, a cup tie, or a friendly match, they always do their best to win – at least, the committee informed the press so a few weeks ago – and it is consequently rather surprising to find that they were beaten by Millwall Athletic on Saturday last by no less than nine goals to one. If this is their true form – and who dare deny it in face of their committee's assertions – the sooner they look out for more new players the better.

14 DECEMBER 1896

CHRISTMAS GIFTS

● Most of our readers give at least one present to a friend at Christmas time, and we should like to recommend that the following souvenirs be given to the persons mentioned:-

• The Argus – a bushel of new adjectives.
• 'Argus, Junior' – medal for impartial criticism (presented by Jack Devey).
• Dr. W. G. Grace – An essay on 'Sportsmanship.'
• J. W. Crabtree – The captaincy of the Aston Villa team.
• Mr. W. McGregor – A League team composed of Liberals.
• John Reynolds – Fresh (h)air.
• Charlie Athersmith – An international cap.
• Dennis Hodgetts – A few hints on 'How to play football.'
• The Aston Unity 'amateurs' – Wages.
• Jimmy Cowan – the Powderhall handicap.
• Johnny Campbell – A bottle of 'Anti-Fat.'
• Aston Villa Reserves – A few victories.
• Mr. W. Shillcock – The new English Cup.
• Jimmy Elliot – A successful benefit.

BRIEFLETS...

☞ *Dennis Hodgetts has won the toss in every match since he joined Small Heath.*

☞ *Rideout, of Aston Villa Reserves, has been transferred to Hereford Thistle. He will not be greatly missed, neither would some of the other reserve forwards were they to depart.*

☞ *Small Heath and the Villa play a friendly game at Perry Barr on Tuesday, the 29th inst., for the benefit of James Elliott, whose state of health precludes him taking an active part in football at the present time.*

☞ *Becton played for Liverpool again on Saturday, and signalised his reappearance with the team by scoring three goals.*

DENNIS HODGETTS

away. A nice pass by Athersmith was only just missed by Smith, who was a few inches over the line when he got the ball in front of goal. Benwell saved cleverly twice, and then Adlington got down and put the ball across in good style, but Spencer cleared, and the Villa forced two corners without securing any tangible advantage. Benwell on one occasion throwing out cleverly. Then the Rangers came down, and a good shot by H. Smith forced Whitehouse to throw out. Benwell at the other end following suit from a long shot by Crabtree. Devey did some nice work in the centre, but shot over the bar. A little later, however, the Villa came again, and after some pretty passing on the left Wheldon put the ball to Reynolds, who transferred to Cowan, he in turn passing to Devey, who with a clever screw shot scored the first goal, giving Benwell no chance. The Rangers stuck to their guns pluckily, and forced a corner on the left, but Welford cleared easily, and Wheldon taking up the attack shot into Benwell's hands. A corner followed, but the ball was got away, and after some good work by the home forwards Jackson put in a rattling good shot, which Whitehouse had to fist out. Griffiths sent in another long one, but Welford cleared, and Cowan at the other end sent in two grand shots. Benwell saving the first in beautiful style. The latter also stopped a terrific shot from Crabtree, but with a long kick Welford put the Villa on the attack again by forcing a corner. Nothing came of it, however, as after some interesting play in front of the goal Crabtree shot right over the centre of the bar. A lovely run and centre by Wigley was applauded, especially as Jackson met the ball and shot right across the goal mouth, the ball going just outside the post. The Villa at once went up field, and from a beautiful centre by Athersmith Smith scored a fine goal. A moment later, from a clever piece of work on the right, followed by some sure work in the centre by Crabtree, Wheldon put on the third goal, the interval arriving with the score – Villa, 3 goals; Berwick Rangers, 0.

On the restart the Villa at once attacked, and Wheldon tried two beautiful shots, which Benwell saved in clever style. Adlington made a tricky run, beating two men smartly, but his final shot was yards wide. Benwell then saved capitally from Athersmith, and afterwards from Crabtree, but the visitors were not to be denied, and from a nice centre by Smith, Crabtree scored with a good shot. Still playing up with spirit Purslow made a nice run, and passed to Jackson, but he was pulled up by Welford, and Crabtree and Wheldon, going down field, a timely pass was made to Devey, who ran through and scored the fifth goal. Welford, feeling his ankle weak, left the field, and the Rangers, playing up in determined fashion, Jackson scored with a rattling shot. After this, although playing a man short, the Villa had the best of the play, but no more goals were scored. Benwell playing exceptionally well and stopping some fine shots. The game thus ended in a win for the Villa by 5 goals to 1.

Berwick Rangers: Benwell; Bevan and Reynolds; Griffiths, Smith and Jolly; Adlington, Jackson, Higgins, Purslow and Wigley.

Aston Villa: Whitehouse; Spencer and Welford; Chatt, Cowan and Reynolds; Athersmith, Devey, Crabtree, Wheldon and Smith.

LEAGUE DIVISION ONE

Saturday 19th December 1896
VILLA 3, NOTTINGHAM F. 2

● The weather was very cold, and there were not more than 6,000 or 7,000 spectators to see the League match between the Villa and Notts Forest. The ground was hard and slippery. Both sides were well represented, though the Forest were minus Adam Scott and the Villa without Welford and Campbell.

The Villa, who kicked off, had two fouls given against them, but they were unproductive, and when Devey and Athersmith came down the right the former ran the ball out. Crabtree tried a good shot which was

ASTON VILLA RESERVE V HEREFORD

● At Perry Barr. The first half was well contested. Hereford, however, had much the better of the game, and Wilkes gave a capital display of goal-keeping. Both Watkins and Lewis, however, succeeded in beating him, and the Villa failed to score. The second half was slightly in favour of the Villa, but their shooting was most erratic. Result:- Hereford Town, 2 goals; Aston Villa Reserve, 0.

MINE HOST AT THE HOLTE

● Mr. J. T. Lees, so well known in connection with the executive of the Villa, has been invited by Messrs Flower to take up the management of the Holte Hotel and the Lower Grounds when the famous football club move to the new home. No one in Birmingham has had so much experience in this particular line as Mr Lees, and Messrs Flower will be fortunate if they can persuade him to undertake the work.

J. T. LEES

DEVEY 'ILLUMINATED'

● Last evening a smoking concert was held at the Olde Royal Hotel, Temple Row, and the testimonial raised on behalf of John Devey, captain of the Aston Villa Football Club, presented to him in recognition of his services to the club during the last six years. It will be remembered that a benefit match was played at Perry Barr between the Villa and Derby County on October 5, the proceeds of which, coupled with the subscription list promoted under the treasurership of Mr. Joseph Dunkley, resulted in upwards of £200 being realised. The testimonial last evening took the form of an illuminated address recording the services of Devey in the football field, and a cheque for £100, this being the amount of the subscription. The address was written by Mr. John Adams, and illuminated in most artistic style by Mr 'Olly' Whateley, one of the oldest of the Villa players. Mr Joseph Dunkley, the hon. treasurer of the fund, presided.

RAINING BUCKETS AT BURNLEY

● Aston Villa had a fruitless journey to Burnley last week, the rain preventing the League match between the clubs being brought to a conclusion. Although unsatisfactory in other respects it is pleasing to note that the Villa were leading at the time the game was abandoned. The date for the re-playing of the match has not yet been fixed, but when the Villa visit Burnley again they will probably have a harder task to win than they would have had on Saturday had the game been played to a finish, for the East Lancashire club are greatly strengthening their team, and when all the new players have settled down the team will be a far more formidable one than it is at present.

JUST IN CASE...

● Under ordinary circumstances, the Aston Villa second team would defeat Berwick Rangers at Worcester, but, determined to leave nothing to chance, the Villa sent their full League team over to the cathedral city on Monday to play the Rangers in the Birmingham Cup competition. Although the home club – for whom Benwell and Purslow, erstwhile Villans, played – gave a plucky display, they proved no match for the League Champions, who romped home easy winners by five goals to one.

over the bar, and then from a foul against Richards, well placed by Evans, Crabtree headed back, and Reynolds scored with a fine shot five minutes from the start. The visitors immediately retaliated, a foul at the other end enabling Adrian Capes to equalise within a minute. The game was fast and interesting, and Wheldon and Devey both tried good shots, but found Allsopp reliable. At length, however, Evans placed the ball well in front and Devey, heading into the net, placed the Villa in front. Cowan sent in a good one, and both Reynolds and Chatt were noticeable for excellent work, the home team at this time having the best of the exchanges. Twice the visiting goal had lucky escapes from Devey, who was in capital form, but nothing more was done up to the interval, when the Villa were leading by 2 goals to 1.

In the second half the Forest were the first to attack, and Whitehouse had all his work cut out to clear from McPherson, Richards rushing up and putting the ball over. Away went Smith, who cleverly beat Ritchie, and shot into goal; Allsopp half-cleared from Devey, but before he could get the ball away Athersmith dashed in and put the Villa further ahead. For a time

James Whitehouse

the home team had the best of it, but gradually the Forest improved, and their forwards made things very warm for the Villa defence. Reynolds and Wheldon only just missed scoring, and then from a corner the ball was screwed into the Villa net, but, after consulting the linesman, the goal was not allowed on the plea that the ball had touched no one. Playing up, the Villa put the ball into the Forest net from a free kick, but it had touched no one, and then the Forest got down, and from a corner Frank Forman scored. From this point the visitors made desperate efforts to get on terms, having considerably the best of the play. A grand shot by Richards was only a few inches wide, but they could not score again, and the Villa won a keen and interesting match by 3 goals to 2.

Notts Forest: Allsopp; Ritchie and Iremonger; Frank Forman, McPherson and Stewart; Fred Forman, Adrian Capes, Richards, Arthur Capes and McInnes.

Aston Villa: Whitehouse; Spencer and Evans; Chatt, Cowan and Reynolds; Athersmith, Devey, Crabtree, Wheldon and Smith.

DIVISION ONE	P	W	L	D	F	A	Pt
Aston Villa	15	10	2	3	34	17	23
Bolton Wanderers	15	9	2	4	28	14	22
Liverpool	18	8	6	4	28	19	20
Preston North End	15	7	3	5	33	22	19
Derby County	16	7	6	3	38	29	17
West Brom	17	6	6	5	16	18	17
Sheffield United	13	5	2	6	19	13	16
Sheffield Wednesday	16	5	5	6	22	24	16
Everton	15	6	6	3	25	22	15
Notts Forest	16	5	6	5	27	23	15
Blackburn Rovers	16	6	7	3	16	23	15
Wolverhampton W.	15	4	7	4	19	17	12
Bury	14	3	5	6	18	26	12
Stoke	17	5	10	2	26	43	12
Sunderland	16	2	9	5	12	26	9
Burnley	14	2	8	4	17	32	8

AWKWARD QUESTION

● How do the Aston Villa directors relish the refusal of the English Football Association to have the international match, England v Scotland, played at their new ground next year?

REMEMBER ME?

● The Burnley people have never quite forgiven Crabtree for deserting their club to join the League Champions, and on Saturday they howled and jeered every time he made the slightest mistake, in a manner calculated to upset the nerve of the stoutest-hearted player. However, he had his revenge, for, shortly before the cessation of hostilities, he scored a magnificent goal, giving the Villa the lead. The spectators appeared to think, and certainly hoped, that their old favourite had lost some of his ability, but they were speedily undeceived.

WE LIKE MONDAYS!

● Monday was a great day with the Aston Villa players. In the afternoon they appeared at Worcester, defeating Berwick Rangers in the first round of the Birmingham Cup to the tune of five goals to one. Having settled that little matter, the Villa players came back to Birmingham, and were greeted with the joyful news that they had been favoured with good luck in the first round of the English Cup competition, Newcastle United having to pay a visit to Perry Barr. Then came the 'smoker' at the Olde Royal, when Jack Devey, the respected captain, was duly presented with the testimonial which has been raised for him recently, and the usual speeches, songs, and 'drinks' followed. It was truly a day to be remembered, and the same remark will apply to the headaches of some of those present the next morning.

NO POINTS FOR PLUM-PUDDING

● The Villa's holiday programme is by no means a light one; they play Liverpool on Christmas Day, and Wolverhampton Wanderers on Boxing Day, and as both games are played away from home, the players must be kept free from all Christmas festivities, for too much plum-pudding often means the loss of points, and the Villa cannot afford to throw anything away at the present time.

REF – RIGHT OR WRONG?

● Aston Villa had a stroke of really bad luck on Saturday, their long journey to Burnley and half an hour's play in the soaking rain going for nothing, the game being abandoned. As this was the only match in the League not brought to a conclusion, although the rain was pretty general, the inference is that either Burnley had a more generous allowance from the watering-pot or that Mr. Armitt is more susceptible to damp than the majority of referees, a conclusion we should be sorry to entertain. There is a disposition in some quarters to blame the referee for stopping the game after having permitted it to begin, the critics arguing that the conditions were no worse when the players left the ground than when they went on, but there is always a disposition when they start to give the weather a chance of showing better behaviour, and when that hope had to be abandoned, Mr. Armitt would certainly remember how severely the referee in the Villa v Sheffield United match of two years ago was blamed for permitting the game to be played out, the conditions being similar, and several of the Sheffield men being laid up for weeks in consequence. Football is not a fine weather game, and the players are generally willing to face all that comes, but there is no good to be gained by subjecting them to the chances of rheumatism or pneumonia, which ninety minutes spent in a storm of sleet with practically no clothes on would entail.

LEAGUE DIVISION ONE

Friday 25th December 1896

LIVERPOOL 3, VILLA 3

● This League match, which has been eagerly anticipated by the followers of football in Liverpool, was played at Anfield Road, yesterday afternoon, in beautiful weather, and in the presence of fully 25,000 spectators.

Allen kicked off for Liverpool, and immediately the ball, by some clever passing, was worked towards the Villa goal, and a magnificent shot by Becton missed by inches only. Play was fast as could be, and a moment later Reynolds shot hard, but was unfortunate in that his shot just skimmed the bar. Even play followed, and then the ball was worked beautifully down by McVean and Michael, and intercepting an accurate pass from the former Becton nipped in and scored with a shot which gave Whitehouse no chance whatever. From the kick-off the Villans once again forged ahead, and Storer was tested by Athersmith, but cleared in style. The pace continued fast, the visitors having somewhat the better of the exchanges for a time. The turn of Liverpool came again, however, but Bradshaw spoiled a lovely chance by getting into an offside position. The backs of both teams were playing a magnificent game, but Bradshaw got the better of Spencer, and put in a well judged centre, which was met by Michael, who when he had the goal at his mercy got his toe under the ball, and kicked high over the bar. From the kick-off a fine concerted movement brought the ball into the Liverpool quarters, and Athersmith receiving from Devey shot into Storer's hands. Then the ball was worked down by Bradshaw, but he was tackled by Spencer, who punted strongly into midfield. The home lads, however, were not to be denied, and Allan, dodging both the Villa backs, scored number two, amid the greatest enthusiasm. This served to rouse the visitors to even greater efforts, which were soon rewarded by a goal from the foot of Cowan – a result which was owing to clever work on the part of the whole of the Villa half-backs. From hands Spencer kicked well up, and Campbell sent in a shot which just skimmed the upright, Athersmith having the same ill-luck a moment later. The Villans kept up the attack, and shot after shot was rained upon Storer by both forwards and half-backs, Wheldon eventually equalising with a shot that might easily have been saved. Still was the game fought in the vicinity of the Liverpool goal. The visitors were unfortunate indeed in not increasing their score. Campbell, when in a fine position, was nicely robbed by Goldie, and then Bradshaw forced a corner, which was easily cleared. A foul let in the Liverpool men, and Niell sent in a fast shot, which Whitehouse with difficulty diverted over the bar. Then came half-time, with the score 2 each.

From the restart, Allan initiated an attack on the Villa's goal, but Michael, with only the goalkeeper in front of him, shot weakly, and the ball was easily got away. The game was not by any means so fast as in the initial half, the pace having evidently told on both teams, and incidents of moment were at this stage but few, the most important, perhaps, being a beautiful centre from the foot of McVean, an effort which, however, resulted in nought. It was here that an incident occurred which again gave Liverpool the lead. A nicely-judged pass of McVean's was headed into goal by Allan, and one of the visitors' half-backs fisted the ball out. There were immediate claims for a penalty kick, but it was only after consulting both linesmen that the referee allowed the appeal. The shot taken by Becton was nicely judged, and scored amidst tremendous cheering. The excitement was now intense, and the visitors once again commenced to do their utmost to get on level terms. Their passing was of the best, their tackling excellent, and their shots straight and true, but the defence of the homesters was sound, and could not be penetrated. At last came a stinging shot from the half-back line, and Storer fumbled the ball, it was bustled through – a well-deserved and hard tried for goal. The remaining play was all in front of the Villa,

RESERVES AT WORCESTER ROVERS

● At Worcester, before fewer than 1,000 spectators. The Rovers commenced the attack, but were pulled up for offside, and after a corner at the Rovers' end, and Field had hit the upright, the same player got in a nice centre, which Harvey received and scored. The Villa, assisted by a strong wind, had the best of play for a time, but Barnett was given plenty to do, and at last, from a centre by Fountain, Newall headed in and equalised. The Villa had rather the best of matters to half-time. Early in the second half the Rovers missed a good chance, and after they had had a few more tries play went to the other end, and Harvey scored with a long shot. Archer adding another within a minute. The Rovers then attacked vigorously, and Newall scored, encouraged by which the Rovers played a determined game, and had the best of the attack to the end, though Harris added another for the Villa. Result:- Villa, 4 goals; Rovers, 2.

VILLA IN THE PICTURE

● I have just seen an advance copy of the first number of the 'Daily Gazette' Penny Portfolio of Eminent Footballers. It contains group portraits of the Aston Villa and Small Heath teams, together with 22 photos of the individual players in each club. The portraits are triumphs of artistic reproduction, and should be in the possession of every lover of the game.

BRIEFLET

☞ Aston Villa, ever on the look out for promising juniors, have just signed up Garrity, of Lozells.

SO WHAT'S NEW?

● The decision of the English Football Association to have the Scotland v England international match played in London has caused great disappointment in local football circles, for there has been so much talk about the game being played on Aston Villa's new ground at the Lower Grounds that in some quarters it was considered as good as settled. But it was a great mistake: the English Association like to know something about the grounds on which their important games are to be decided, and Birmingham will have to wait for at least another two years.

ELLIOTT BENEFIT

● It is to be hoped that the football enthusiasts of Birmingham will assemble in large numbers at Perry Barr on Tuesday next, the 29th inst., when the Villa will oppose Small Heath for the benefit of James Elliott, a player who rendered the League Champions such service a couple of seasons ago, but whose health is precarious at the present time that it is doubtful if he will ever be able to play football again. If ever a player deserved a bumping benefit, Elliott does, for it is in consequence of taking part in the winter pastime which delights so many thousands of people that he has been so ill. I am sure all my readers will heartily re-echo my wish that he may soon be restored to the best of health, and that he will clear a substantial sum from next Tuesday's match. The

JAMES ELLIOTT

who looked for a time likely winners, but the whistle blew with the score 3 all.

Liverpool: Storer; Goldie and Wilkie; McCartney, Neill and Cleghorn; McVean, Michael, Allan, Becton and Bradshaw.

Villa: Whitehouse; Crabtree and Spencer; Reynolds, Cowan and Chatt; Smith, Wheldon, Campbell, Devey and Athersmith.

LEAGUE DIVISION ONE

Saturday 26th December 1896
WOLVES 1, VILLA 2

● The contest was brought off at Molineux Grounds, before a crowd of about 18,000 people, notwithstanding that the morning did not open any too brightly, rain falling heavily till within an hour or two of the commencement of the contest. The Villa had the same team as drew with Liverpool on the previous day, and the Wanderers made no alteration in their eleven.

The ground was heavy, and the Wanderers, winning the toss, started with their backs to the hotel. The Villa immediately began to press, their passing being excellent, especially considering the state of the turf. Wheldon put in a good shot, but Tennant saved, and after consistent attacking by the visitors, Wheldon again tried for goal. He put in a fine shot, but Tennant again saved. The Wanderers made a brief rush now and again, but there was no mistaking the superiority of the Villa. Griffiths just stopped Athersmith, and from a free kick the ball was afterwards sent in front of the Wanderers' goal. Here Chatt shot hard, and the ball, touching Owen, went into the net. Tonks went to the other end after the restart, and centreing well gave Miller an opportunity, which was not taken. The attack was not sustained, and the Villa going to the other end, Campbell hit the crossbar with a hard shot. A centre into

Bob Chatt

goal gave Tennant and Eccles some trouble, and there was a sharp contest on the line, but the ball was forced into the net, making the second point for the Villa. Soon after this Malpass headed into the net from a free kick, and subsequently the game became more even. The Villa, however, had the best of it, though they could not score again, and half-time came with Aston Villa leading by 2 goals to 1.

The Wanderers were the first to press after the kick off, but Athersmith got away, though his centre was not taken advantage of. Then the Wolves forced a corner, but this was cleared, and soon after they gained a free kick, which produced some danger. The ball was got away, and a little later Cowan sent in a magnificent shot. Tennant tried to stop it, and diverted its course, the ball striking the crossbar and going into play. The appeal of the Villa for a goal was disregarded. The Wanderers made some dangerous rushes, and time after time it looked as if they would break through, Smith missed an opportunity by sending out, and twice Crabtree cleared from close attacks. Eccles stopped a run to the other end, and then Whitehouse saved from Owen. The Villa custodian had some work to do about this time, but he managed to keep his goal intact. Smith was injured, and the Wolves appealed for a penalty, but the referee and linesmen on consultation declined to allow it. Miller gave Whitehouse a warm shot to deal with, especially as McMain and Smith went for the goalkeeper at the same time. McMain was hurt, but soon recovered, and to the end the Wanderers pressed. There was, however, no alteration in the score, the result being:- Aston Villa, 2; Wolverhampton Wanderers, 1.

Wolverhampton Wanderers: Tennant; Eccles and Wood; Griffiths, Malpass and Owen; Tonks, Lyden, McMain, Smith and Miller.

Aston Villa: Whitehouse; Spencer and Crabtree; Chatt, Cowan and Reynolds; Athersmith, Devey, Campbell, Wheldon, and Smith.

game should be much more interesting than the average 'friendlies' are, for Dennis Hodgetts and Charlie Hare will be playing against their old club for the first time, and both players will assuredly do their best to defeat their comrades of days gone by.

ALL ABOUT JAMES

● Thinking that a brief account of Elliott's football career would be interesting to those who peruse this page, I called on that player the other day, and he willingly obliged me with particulars. James Alexander Elliott – for that is his full name – was born at Barrhead, near Glasgow, on October 20th, 1869, being now in his twenty-eighth year. As a youngster he was exceedingly fond of athletic recreation, and at the age of sixteen was a prominent member of Barrhead Rangers, while a little later he threw in his lot with the Barrhead Artillery club, the leading club of the district. In 1889 he was booked, by means of an agent, for the Middlesbrough Ironopolis club, and, playing at right half-back, aided that club to secure the Cleveland Charity Cup during his first season with the team. The following year he was moved to right full back, where he partnered Langley (now of Sheffield Wednesday.) After three seasons with the 'Nops' he was induced to join Aston Villa, and during the 1893-4 season he and Johnny Baird were generally considered to be the two best backs in the Midlands. In addition to being a first-class footballer, Elliott has also excelled in other branches of sport, and in 1890 he won the second prize for pole-jumping at the Highland gathering at Middlesbrough, with a jump of 9ft. 6in. Both on and off the field he is a thorough gentleman, and has made numerous friends since he came to Birmingham. Therefore do not forget the Christmas toast: 'Success to Elliott's benefit!'

VILLA GO TOP

● Top of the League at last! Aston Villa have been doing wonderfully well of late, and their supporters have been anxiously awaiting the time when the team would once again be at the head of the League table, but it was not generally expected that they would gain the coveted position on Saturday last, for few anticipated that Bolton Wanderers would prove unequal to the task of defeating West Bromwich Albion at Burnden Park, but it was so, and as the Villa took two points from Notts County the same day, the Perry Barr club now possesses the best record of any club in either division of the League, which is a source of great joy to all Birmingham people.

SURPRISE, SURPRISE...

● Aston Villa Reserves actually won a match away from home last week, defeating Worcester Rovers by four goals to two. This was a greater surprise than the much talked-of earthquake!

BIRMINGHAM AND DISTRICT LEAGUE

	P	W	L	D	F	A	Pts
Wolverhampton Wanderers	16	13	2	1	55	15	27
Hereford Thistle	12	10	1	1	40	10	21
Small Heath	16	8	4	4	46	30	20
Aston Villa	17	7	4	6	32	21	20
Kidderminster Harriers	13	7	3	3	31	18	17
Shrewsbury Town	15	6	6	3	38	37	15
Berwick Rangers	13	5	4	4	27	23	14
Halesowen	15	6	8	1	28	50	13
Stourbridge	13	4	5	4	30	26	12
Hereford	13	5	6	2	29	23	12
Brierley Hill Alliance	13	5	7	1	21	33	11
Worcester Rovers	12	4	5	3	26	35	11
West Bromwich Albion	14	4	7	3	23	33	11
Singer's	11	3	6	2	16	24	8
Oldbury Town	15	1	10	4	12	38	6
Redditch Town	15	1	11	3	30	69	5

JAMES ELLIOTT BENEFIT

Tuesday 29th December 1896
VILLA 1, SMALL HEATH 1

● A friendly match was played between these teams at Perry Barr yesterday, for the benefit of J. Elliott, who a couple of seasons ago was a useful and plucky back in the Villa team, but is now, from illness, incapacitated from following the game.

There was a capital attendance, some 4,000 or 5,000 spectators being present, so that the benefit should prove a good one. Both clubs were well represented, though on the Villa side Field played outside right instead of Athersmith, whilst the Heathens gave a trial to Groves, a soldier, on the outside left. Small Heath had the wind and hill in their favour, and some interesting exchanges took place. The Villa were evidently not over-exerting themselves, being content for the most part to take things easily. Just before half-time the Heathens made a strong attack, and, though Whitehouse half cleared a warm shot, Groves met the ball on the rebound and put it into the net, the visitors thus leading at the interval by 1 goal to 0.

In the second half play was of an open character, each side pressing in turn. Then the Villa came down with a rush, and from a good centre by Field, Wheldon shot hard and fast for goal, Pointer, though he fumbled the ball, bringing off a good save. Wheldon made another nice dribble, though closely pressed by Farnall, but he shot wide, and then, when Devey cleverly got through his men, he was stopped by Pratt. Immediately afterwards Wheldon again got through his opponents, but with the goal absolutely at his mercy shot outside. Small Heath ran up, and got a foul for 'hands'

John Reynolds

right in front of the posts, but Reynolds cleared, and Smith ran down the left, but only to put his centre over the bar. From a throw-in Smith got a nice chance, but only forced an unproductive corner. Chatt pulled up the visitors' left, and the Villa were soon pressing again, though they were palpably not trying too hard. Crabtree and Wheldon both put the ball out. There was an exciting scrimmage from a foul under the Small Heath bar, but the ball was got away, and two corners to the Villa were unproductive. The home goal had a

BOASTING IN VAIN

● The doings of the Aston Villa team during the holiday season of course claim first attention, and though it is too late to write much about their excellent displays at Liverpool and Wolverhampton, where they gained three points out a possible four on successive days, it is certainly not too late to congratulate the players on the brilliant performances. To make a draw at Anfield Road with the Liverpool team was perhaps the most creditable achievement of the two, for last season's champions of the Second League had been carrying everything before them in fine style, and had been bragging loudly as to how they were going to defeat the Villa. Their boasting was in vain, however, though it cannot be denied that they did well to score three goals against the present leaders, a performance which only one other League club (West Bromwich Albion) had accomplished this season. Becton evidently meant showing the Villa what he could do, for he played in irresistible style, and scored two of the three goals obtained by his side.

ALBION AGAIN

● In the second round of the Birmingham Cup competition the Villa are drawn against West Bromwich Albion, the game to be played on the Stoney Lane ground on Monday, the 25th inst. As the Throstles have already defeated their doughty opponents twice this season – in a League game and for the Staffordshire Cup – it will be interesting to note if they manage the trick for the third time. Should they succeed once again, the Albion will be entitled to every credit for a brilliant achievement, for the Villa are the present holders of the Birmingham Cup, and do not mean losing it if they can possibly help it.

CUP CLAIM

● "Nothing can prevent Aston Villa keeping the League Cup in their possession for at least another twelve months," remarks an athletic contemporary. What has the man who stole the English Cup to say on the subject?

GATE GLOOM

● While Aston Villa are delighting their numerous supporters by their brilliant displays both at home and away, there is a very different story to relate concerning the doings of their near neighbours and erstwhile rivals, Small Heath. Although the team has been materially altered since the commencement of the season, new players having been brought from all parts of the kingdom, little if any improvement has been manifested in their play, and it is very evident that unless the club secure a few victories during the next few weeks they will have no following worth mentioning left. The 'gates' at the Coventry Road ground have been growing less and less each week, and on Boxing Day, when Edinburgh Hibernians were playing the Heathens, there were barely three thousand spectators.

PATH TO OBLIVION

● Small Heath are on the broad and easy path which leads to oblivion; they could do no more than draw against Walsall, while the Edinburgh Hibernians made rings round them. These last, however, were far too good a team for Small Heath, their combination being of the Villa class, and it is a great pity we can't see them at Perry Barr. The committee are trying Hare at centre-forward, and he shapes very well, giving Hodgetts some much needed support. However, defenders are what the team badly needs, and until two or three good men are procured in this department Small Heath will continue to descend.

narrow escape, and from another corner forced by Smith, Reynolds headed out, and though still pressing, the Villa could not score, Campbell skimming the bar. At length, however, from a beautiful centre by Devey, Smith headed into the net. The home team continued to attack, but nothing more was scored, and the game ended in a draw of 1 goal each.

Small Heath: Pointer; Lester and Pratt; Farnall, Thomas and Walton; Inglis, Jones, Robertson, Hodgetts and Groves.

Aston Villa: Whitehouse; Spencer and Crabtree; Chatt, Cowan and Reynolds; Field, Devey, Campbell, Wheldon and Smith.

LEAGUE DIVISION ONE
Saturday 2nd January 1897
VILLA 0, BURNLEY 3

● This match was played at Perry Barr in fine, frosty weather, before a crowd of about 12,000 or 14,000 persons. The ground was frozen and slippery. Burnley played their two recent captures from Wolverhampton, and the Villa were without Crabtree and Welford, Devey also being on the sick list, but consenting to play in the absence of a substitute.

The home team played uphill against a slight breeze, but were the fist to threaten danger, Wheldon only just shooting outside. At the other end Bowes speedily called on Whitehouse, and it soon became evident that the Villa were not in their happiest mood and where not going to have things all their own way. On the other hand, the Burnley men kept their feet much better than their opponents, and frequently threatened danger, only the fine defence of Spencer stopping them on several occasions. Fouls for hands gave the visitors a couple of chances, and before the game was ten minutes old they had drawn first blood, Black forcing the ball into the net through Whitehouse's hands. Black was not off-side, but the two men who played the ball immediately before him where, though the referee allowed the goal. Campbell and Wheldon then narrowly missed the Burnley goal, and from a shot by Reynolds, Tatham effected a lucky save. Burnley forced  a corner, and the Villa were fortunate to get out of danger, whilst Devey, with the opposing goal open, shot over the bar. Campbell made a fine run, but there was no one to help him, and just as Wheldon was about to shoot from a centre by Athersmith, he was knocked off the ball by Dunn, the interval arriving with the score: Burnley, 1 goal; Villa, 0.

Fred Wheldon

In the second half the home team had considerably the best of the play, but though they were very unlucky in not scoring, they did not play in anything like their usual form, Spencer and Campbell being the only ones to do themselves justice. On the other hand, Tatham kept goal magnificently, brought off several remarkably fine saves, whilst the whole of the visitors worked hard and were always on the ball. From corners the Villa twice headed just over the bar, whilst at the other end a very bad mistake by Evans let in Toman, who had no difficulty in beating Whitehouse a second time. Three times in rapid succession Tatham saved on the line, whilst Campbell tried to rush him through, and then, breaking away again, Bowes scored, Whitehouse evidently misjudging the shot. Burnley thus won by 3 goals to 0, and thoroughly deserved their victory.

Burnley: Tatham; Dunn and McLintock; Place (sen), Longhair and Taylor; Beveridge, Black, Toman and Place (jun).

Aston Villa: Whitehouse; Spencer and Evans; Chatt, Cowan and Reynolds; Athersmith, Devey, Campbell, Wheldon,and Smith.

OFF-DAY AT HOME

● It has often been said that "it is the unexpected that happens at football," and the truth of this remark was never more verified than on Saturday last, when Burnley – the 'wooden spoonists' of the League – defeated Aston Villa, admittedly the most brilliant combination of football players of the present day, on their own ground by three goals to nothing. It was indeed a great surprise, and the local papers have made much of it, some critics ascribing it to one cause and some to another. There is nothing to go into hysterics over, however, for the Villa have played so consistently well throughout the season that one can forgive them having an off-day just for once in a while. Their record is still by far the best of any club in the First Division of the League, and the probability of their again carrying off the Championship is in no way decreased by the unexpected reverse which they received at the hands of the Burnley club. Still, it would not do for those little surprises to happen too often, but with Crabtree and Welford back again in the team it is scarcely likely that they will experience such another heavy defeat on their own ground for a long time to come.

HAIL THE HEATHENS!

● Now we shan't be long! Small Heath have actually won another League match, and away from home, too. Their victims were Gainsborough Trinity, who had only been defeated once previously on their own ground for two seasons, so the Heathens are entitled to every credit for their victory.

WALTON BENEFIT

● On Monday next William Howard Walton, the well-known and highly-esteemed Small Heath player, takes a benefit, Aston Villa visiting the Coventry Road ground to play a friendly match with the Heathens. Walton has been connected with the club since 1888, and has rendered good service to them for over eight years.

REPORTERS BEWARE

● There was a rumour current in local football circles last week that Aston Villa were endeavouring to secure Divers, the Celtic forward who was recently suspended indefinitely because he refused to play unless certain reporters were excluded from the ground. How Messrs Jones, Doe, and Clucas must have trembled in their shoes when they heard that that player might possibly leave his home in Glasgow to take up his quarters in Birmingham! Doubtless they wondered how the Villa committee would act if they were placed in the same predicament as the Celts recently were. However, their alarm was needless, for Divers is not coming to the Villa, and the local football scribes can continue to say whatever they please – in their usual fair manner of course – until some of the adversely criticised players happen to meet them one dark night, and then – but it's too awful to contemplate.

BRIEFLETS...

↪ *J. Reader, the Albion goalkeeper, is to have a benefit this season. He is endeavouring to get Aston Villa to visit West Bromwich on Easter Tuesday.*

↪ *Evans, who played at left back for the Villa last week, is a native of Barnard Castle, Durham, the district from which Welford hails.*

↪ *The Villa play Sunderland next Saturday; they have never won a League match at Wearside.*

↪ *A match has been made for C. Athersmith (Aston Villa) to give G. Anderson (Blackburn Rovers) three yards start in 110 yards for £50 a side.*

LEAGUE DIVISION ONE

Saturday 9th January 1897

SUNDERLAND 4, VILLA 2

● The Villa made their annual trip to Wearside to play the first of their two matches against Sunderland. Unfortunately the visitors were short of Devey, Reynolds, and Welford, which caused an entire re-arrangement of their team, Crabtree going forward, and Burton and Evans being brought in, though the latter was suffering from an injured jaw, the result of a severe knock in the Burnley match.

Half a gale, accompanied by a slight fall of snow, was blowing up the field, but there were 7,000 or 8,000 spectators present. The Villa won the toss, and took advantage of the wind, but the home team were the first to press, and within three minutes Gillespie headed into the net from a corner, the Villa defence being very shaky. The visitors were a long time settling down, and made but poor use of the wind, the forwards trying too much close passing, and, the left wing of defence being very poor, Spencer frequently had to cover both sides of the field. Campbell tried a long shot, which only just missed, and Doig brought off fine saves from Wheldon and Campbell. A couple of corners to the Villa were unproductive, but from a foul they ought to have scored, Burton when in a grand position putting the ball over the bar. Sunderland played in grand style, and were frequently dangerous, their half-backs supporting the forwards most effectively, whilst Gow and McNeil were generally given plenty of space to clear in. Another fine shot by Campbell was cleverly saved by Doig, and directly afterwards the same player headed in, but only for Doig to put it over the bar. Sunderland pressed, but Athersmith got away and, beating Gow in clever fashion, centred right in front of goal. Doig half cleared, but with Smith in attendance, he put the ball to Ferguson, who headed into his own net, the half-time score being 1 goal each.

The commencement of the second half was very sensational, for within a couple of minutes, from a fine piece of play by Athersmith, a desperate bully was fought in front of the home goal, Crabtree eventually putting the ball into the net. The Villa, however, did not hold the lead long, for in less than ten minutes Johnston and Gillespie scored again. Whitehouse defending very badly. After this the Villa had considerably the best of the play, the forwards dribbling and passing well, but lacking dash at the finish. Doig was in splendid form, and, though Athersmith time after time beat Gow and centred accurately, there was no one to help him, and the home defenders got the ball away. Just before the close Morgan scored again, and though there was a unanimous appeal for both a foul and offside, the referee, after consulting the linesmen, allowed the point. Sunderland thus winning amidst great enthusiasm by 4 goals to 2.

Sunderland: Doig; McNeil and Gow; Ferguson, Dunlop and Wilson; Gillespie, Harvie, Morgan, Hannah and Johnston.

Aston Villa: Whitehouse; Spencer and Evans; Chatt, Cowan and Burton; Athersmith, Crabtree, Campbell, Wheldon and Smith.

AWKWARD QUESTIONS

● Will Aston Villa gain their first victory at Sunderland tomorrow?
● Why did Cowan not compete for the Powderhall Handicap this year?
● Did the Villa committee refuse to give him leave of absence?
● Did he think it unwise to have another 'injury'?
● When will Johnnie Cowan make his reappearance in the Villa team?

IMAGINE THAT!

● I had the misfortune to attend the Villa v Burnley match in company with an enthusiastic footballer who had not seen the Villa perform before this season, and must confess the experience was not an enviable one. He is connected with a southern team, whose price as a job lot would be less than one of the Villa men, and he was, therefore, very anxious to see the £250 men perform. Well, he saw them, and when he goes back he assures me there will be a considerable rise in the price of men placed on the transfer list in his district. Athersmith was another man he came prepared to be delighted with; he had read so much concerning his electrifying runs that being doubtful of his ability to follow him with the naked eye, he had brought a pair of field glasses with him. He didn't need the glasses for this purpose, but he turned them on the press box with interest, saying he should like to see men with such powerful imaginations as our scribes possess. Of course, I tried to palliate the Villa's misfortune, assuring him that the men, being anxious to see some interest left in the League competition, had been passing the week in celebrating the anniversary of their coup at Powderhall, but as he had paid eighteen-pence to see the show, this didn't please him.

FITNESS PROBLEMS

● The Villa supporters, I find, are not much downcast over the reverse, the lesson administered being considered a fair equivalent for the points. Long continued success had given the men the impression that they were invincible, and a consequent disinclination to train has manifested itself, which the results of Saturday's match will do much to eliminate. They were, besides, practically playing nine men, Devey being too ill to do anything right, and Athersmith wisely reserving himself for his match with Anderson of Blackburn Rovers. It is significant of the dearth of talent, that though the Villa have about eighty men signed on, they have not a single reserve forward fit to put into the first team, and if Devey's health doesn't improve before tomorrow, they are not likely to get points even from Sunderland.

HEATHENS ARE HOPING

● Small Heath have not given many good exhibitions at home this season, and the attendances have gradually been growing less, but it is to be hoped that there will be a big crowd on the Coventry Road ground on Monday, when the Villa oppose the Heathens. It is only a friendly match, but the proceeds are for the benefit of Billy Walton, who has been playing for the Small Heath club for over seven years, and has never once been on the 'black list,' and it would be a thousand pities if so deserving a player were not to make a good thing out of it.

ANOTHER THRASHING?

● After the tremendous thrashing which Small Heath received at Millwall a month ago, one would have thought that the Southerners had seen enough of them for one season. This is not the case, however, for tomorrow they are due at New Brompton to play a friendly game. Will it be another case of nine goals to one?

WALTON BENEFIT MATCH

Monday 11th January 1897
SMALL HEATH 2, VILLA 1

● A friendly match between these clubs was played yesterday at Small Heath for the benefit of Walton, one of the home half-backs, who has done a lot of service for the Heathens during the past few years. Unfortunately, the weather was not very favourable, and the ground, following the snow and thaw, was a perfect quagmire, which made good football impossible, and certainly not very enjoyable to the spectators, of whom about 1,500 were present. Neither club was fully represented, the Villa being short of Athersmith, Devey, Wheldon, Chatt, Reynolds, Crabtree, and Welford, whilst Small Heath had Inglis, Hare, Ison, and Farnall away.

Fred Burton

Small Heath kicked towards the Muntz Street goal during the first half, but, as already indicated, the play was not very high class, and under such conditions as prevailed detailed description is not called for. The Heathens had the best of the exchanges, and Jones and Edwards both got the ball into the Villa net, neither point, however, being allowed owing to infringements of the rules. At the interval, accordingly, no goals had been scored. Some 20 minutes after the game had been resumed Oakes put in a good centre from which Edwards headed into the net past Whitehouse, whilst a few minutes later Oakes added a second point. Just before the close Griffiths scored for the Villa, and the game ended in a win for Small Heath by 2 goals to 1.

Aston Villa: Whitehouse; Spencer and Bourne; Burton, Cowan and Griffiths; Field, Green, Campbell, Harris and Smith.

Small Heath: Pointer; Lester and Pratt; Goode, Leake and Walton; Oakes, Robertson, Jones, Hodgetts and Edwards.

LEAGUE DIVISION ONE

Saturday 16th January 1897
VILLA 2, SUNDERLAND 1

● Favoured by the fine weather there was a large attendance at Perry Barr, quite 15,000 spectators assembling to witness the return match between these clubs. Welford and Whitehouse were out of the home team, whilst in the absence of Hannah and Harvey Sunderland played Hamilton and Campbell. The visitors won the toss and had the wind behind them, despite which, however, the Villa forced the pace, and had the best of the exchanges. Some brilliant work by Wilson, Gow, and Doig, though kept them out, whilst the Sunderland forwards were frequently dangerous, Morgan and Johnstone especially. Spencer and Crabtree were kept busily employed, and the home half-back line assisted the forwards well. Athersmith made some splendid runs and centres, but they were scarcely utilised as they ought to have been. Devey was very clever, and Campbell and Wheldon tried some long shots which Doig smartly saved. Wilkes was also at his best and allowed no liberties to be taken. A grand shot by Wheldon deserved to score, but the ball struck the bar and rebounded, the interval thus arriving without a score on either side. Immediately upon the restart Devey ran up the field and put in a grand shot which Doig was trying to get away when Wheldon dashed up and breasted into the net. The Villa still attacked, forcing a foul and then a corner, but the ball was eventually put behind. Another foul fell to them in a good position, but Chatt fisted the ball into the net and from the free kick the visitors got away, though only for a time, a fine piece of combined play giving Reynolds a shot which went just over the bar, Devey

HAIR-TEARING TIME

● The Villa have lost another match, and their supporters are tearing their hair and predicting all sorts of trouble for the Perry Barr brigade, to the great amusement of the disinterested on-lookers who care more for a good game than to see one club smother all opponents. Up to Christmas the Villa were exceptionally fortunate, their injured list was unimportant, and their defence stronger than usual, and it was lucky for them that it was so, for the forward line compares very unfavourably with the clever string the Villa have generally possessed. A few years ago it was customary to agitate for the selection of the whole of the English-born Villa forwards for the International matches, and we have seen four out of the five playing for the English League and beating the pick of Scotland, but that wouldn't be possible now, for with the exception of Athersmith and Campbell none of them have any chance for international caps. The others are good ordinary players, but that is all."

POOR RESERVE SUPPORT

● If the results of the Villa's last two matches open the eyes of the committee to the need of strengthening the reserve team – not especially to win the Birmingham League, but to have first-class men ready to play in the League team when any of the 'regulars' are unable to turn out – the four points will not have been lost in vain. The Villa reserve team as at present constituted is a weakness to the club, and it is not at all surprising that the average attendance at their matches at Perry Barr is only about five hundred, whereas Small Heath Reserves attract between three and four thousand spectators each week.

SCHOOLBOY STUFF

● Hereford Thistle are not a great team, but they fairly made rings round the Villa Reserves at Perry Barr last week, and thoroughly deserved their three goals to nothing victory. Wilkes kept goal finely for the home team, and Griffiths, who reappeared in the team after three months' absence, played a fairly good game at half, but the others – well, to put it mildly, their display would have disgraced a team of schoolboys, the efforts of the forward line being painfully weak. Why not put the whole front rank on the transfer list?

SOME SUPPORTERS SATISFIED

● It is to be feared that Walton will not realise a very large sum as the result of his benefit match on Monday, for the attendance was by no means a large one. Still, as some players in the district have actually lost money over their 'benefits' – Harry Wood, of Wolverhampton Wanderers, for instance – Walton will probably be content with the £50 odd which he will receive. Although 'full League team' were advertised, Small Heath played three reserve men, while the Villa eleven included no less than six second-teamers. The game was by no means an interesting one to watch, the condition of the ground being against good play, but the Heathens won by two goals to one, so their supporters are probably satisfied with the result.

repeating the operation a moment later. Sunderland then had a turn, Wilkes making a grand save from an off-side shot by Hamilton. Doig at the other end saved finely from a dropping shot, and then Sunderland came down again, Gillespie making a poor finish. The visitors were frequently pulled up for offside, their best efforts in mid-field being spoiled by their front rank getting continually in front of the ball and the Villa backs. A fine shot by Athersmith was well saved by Doig, and Smith was just knocked off the ball in time. The Villa continued to have the best of the play, a splendid try by Wheldon being only a shade wide. Doig made two more good saves. Then a foul against Reynolds for holding gave Sunderland a chance, and the kick being well placed Gillespie headed into the net and made the scores level. Wheldon was badly fouled just in front of goal, and from the scrimmage the ball was rushed into the net, the Villa thus taking the lead once more. The game continued to be exciting, and whilst the visitors forced an unproductive corner Doig had twice to save dangerous shots from Campbell, and Wheldon. No further scoring took place, the Villa winning by 2 goals to 1. Teams:-

Sunderland: Doig; McNeil and Gow; Ferguson, Dunlop, and Wilson; Gillespie, Campbell, Morgan, Johnstone, and Hamilton.

Aston Villa: Wilkes; Spencer and Crabtree, Chatt, Cowan, and Reynolds; Athersmith, Devey, Campbell, Wheldon, and Smith.

Saturday 23rd January 1897
TOTTENHAM 2, VILLA 2

● It has become generally recognised that when Aston Villa go to London they go to play football and not to take a holiday. Therefore it is that they are such a capital 'draw'.

On Saturday they went to play Tottenham Hotspur, and despite the fact that snow was falling thickly about three thousand persons were present to witness the contest. The Villa were strongly represented, but could not beat the home eleven, who had the satisfaction of making a draw of two goals each with the premier combination in the country. Athersmith scored the first goal for the Villa after twenty minutes' play, but Lanham equalised before the interval.

Afterwards each side scored a goal. The visitors delighted the spectators by their clever passing. They did a great deal more attacking than the home players, but the latter were very dangerous when they broke away. Taken as a whole the game was fast and exciting, and the spectators were well pleased with the display.

RETURN TO FORM

● Once again have Aston Villa returned to form, and their display against Sunderland on Saturday last was in every respect an excellent one. True, they only won by two goals to one, but the Wearsiders are by no means the weak team which their poor position in the League table might lead one to suppose, and they played almost as well as they did a couple of seasons ago, when they won the Championship.

WELFORD RESTED

● Jimmy Welford's ankle is still troubling him, and he is not likely to be seen in the team again just yet. This is a pity, for he makes a better partner for Spencer than Crabtree does. All Villa supporters will be glad when he is able to play once again, for Jimmy is very popular with the crowd, and his huge lunges are as much appreciated as his big hits when playing cricket at the County Ground are.

FIRST VISIT FOR SPURS

● According to the League fixture list, Preston North End were to have visited Perry Barr tomorrow. However, as the Prestonians have a Lancashire Cup tie on, the Villa have consented to postpone the League match for a time, and have arranged for Tottenham Hotspur to pay them a visit. The 'Spurs' have never previously been seen in Birmingham, and football enthusiasts in this locality know little of them, except that they were knocked out of the English Cup competition by Luton Town last week to the tune of four goals to nothing. This is no very great recommendation, and as the game is only a 'friendly,' the attendance is scarcely likely to create a record.

DIVERS ON THE WAY?

● The Villa committee are understood to be on the look-out for new players, and a Lancashire paper stated last week that it was highly probable that Divers, the well-known Celtic forward, would shortly come to Birmingham. The Villa certainly might do worse than secure this player; he has made a great reputation in Scotland, and would prove very useful if any of the regular forwards were injured, for John Cowan does not appear to be well enough to play yet awhile, and there is no forward in the reserve team smart enough to be introduced into the League eleven.

RUMOUR UNFOUNDED

● A ridiculous rumour was circulated in Birmingham last week to the effect that Freddy Burton, the Villa reserve half-back, had been transferred to Small Heath. The statement was entirely without foundation, and Burton is naturally greatly annoyed that it should have appeared. It may be worth mentioning that the paper which published the 'news' claims to be 'the best football paper in the Midlands!'

COWAN SHARES WORKLOAD

● James Cowan still plays excellently at centre half-back for the Villa, and it is very seldom indeed that his play is adversely criticised. However, he is scarcely as good as he was three or four seasons back, when he used to do the work of two ordinary players, and was generally considered to be the cleverest player in the Villa team.

JAMES COWAN

Monday 25th January 1897

ALBION 2, VILLA 1

● These clubs met yesterday at Stoney Lane in the second round of the Birmingham Senior Cup Competition. The Albion were fully represented, but the Villa were without Crabtree, Reynolds, and Welford. The weather and ground were quite unfit for football, but the referee (Mr. Barker, of Stoke) decided that the game must be played, and the teams accordingly turned out before 4,000 and 5,000 enthusiastic spectators.

The ground was covered with several inches of snow, and a perfect blizzard of wind and snow blew down the field, the temperature being also intensely cold. The Albion having won the toss, the Villa kicked off uphill against the wind and snow, and were at once pressed, Wilkes bringing off a fine save from a long dropping shot. Richards tried another one at long range, but Wilkes cleverly put it against the post and outside. The Villa ran up on the left, but Smith was stopped by Evans, and the Albion attacked again, Wilkes saving twice in quick succession. Play was quite a farce under the circumstances, anything like ordinary football being out of the question. Why the referee permitted the game to continue goodness only knows. The wind blew the snow down field in sheets, and the players could scarcely stand. At length, after the game had lasted about a quarter of an hour, Cameron scored the first goal for the Albion with a long shot which gave the opposing goalkeeper no chance. Still the Villa were in no sense disconcerted, and as the result of a capital run by the forwards Athersmith centred, and Campbell scored a pretty goal. The

Tom Wilkes

Albion got down again, and quickly took the lead, a fast shot by Watson going into the corner of the net. Another good attempt was made by the Villa right, and Devey's final shot – a good one – was only just wide of the posts. Then a grand piece of play by Griffiths almost ended in his scoring, the ball skimming the bar. For the remainder of the first half the Villa held their own fairly well under the circumstances, and at the interval the Albion crossed over with a lead of 2 goals to 1.

On resuming, the Albion made a good run up the right, and when Wilkes slipped Watson had the goal at his mercy, but missed badly. The Villa pressed, but several times drove the ball outside. They seemed to misjudge the power of the wind entirely, and made poor use of their opportunities. From a beautiful pass by Chatt, Wheldon was left with a good opening, but he shot several yards wide. Devey shot into Reader's hands, and then the Villa failed to improve a nice chance from a foul in front of goal. Perry, who was playing a fine game, repeatedly got his side out of difficulties, and the Villa continued to be weak in front of goal. Richards and Watson made a nice run, but Bassett got offside. Then Williams had to give a corner, but Devey put the ball yards over the bar. Five more corners followed in quick succession, but none of them were improved upon, and Watson, breaking away, took the ball momentarily to the other end. Reader saved a good shot from Wheldon, and then another corner to the Villa was put behind. The visitors continued to have the best of matters right up to the finish, but their shooting was bad, and they failed to add to the score, the game thus ending in a win for the Albion by 2 goals to 1.

West Bromwich Albion: Reader; Evans and Williams; Perry, Higgins and Banks; Bassett, Flewitt, Cameron, Richards and Watson.

Aston Villa: Wilkes; Spencer and Evans; Chatt, Cowan and Griffiths; Athersmith, Devey, Campbell, Wheldon and Smith.

RISING COSTS AT LOWER GROUNDS

● The Aston Villa shareholders seemed a little astonished at the cost of the alterations at the Lower Grounds. £14,000 is certainly a big sum to spend on a football and cycling enclosure, but, believe me, it will be a lot more than that. If they get the ground finished for £18,000 they will be lucky. They despised the warnings "Observer" gave them when the scheme was first mooted; but no matter! We shall see what we shall see. I hear that certain of the leading cycling firms in the Midlands intend combining to build a new cycling track on the most approved lines in Birmingham. There will be some lively competition with the new track at Aston then.

HONOURS EVEN

● Little interest was taken in Aston Villa's visit to the South on Saturday to play a friendly game with Tottenham Hotspur, and the few people who did trouble to enquire for the result were quite satisfied to learn that the game had been drawn.

TRICKY THROSTLES

● Bombshells and dynamite! Here's a surprise, and no mistake! The Villa had been defeated this season in a League match at West Bromwich, and the Albion had also thrown them out of the Staffordshire Cup competition, but no one anticipated that the 'Throstles' would do the trick a third time on Monday, when the teams met in the second round of the Birmingham Cup. But it was so, nevertheless, and there is great joy at West Bromwich in consequence, while all is gloomy at Perry Barr. Sadness reigns supreme!

OPTIMISTIC OPENING DATE

● So it is definitely settled that the Villa are to open their new ground on March 13th, when Liverpool play their League match with the present champions, is it? Well, if one can judge by appearances, the work at the Aston Lower Grounds will not be completed by that time, and it will be poor judgement on the part of the directors if the ground is opened before it is really ready.

PRESS PLEA

● It is to be hoped that the arrangements for the newspaper scribes at the new ground will be of a first-class character, for the reporters at Perry Barr have had a great deal to complain of, and will thankfully welcome an improvement. The Villa could scarcely do better than have a press-box constructed on the same lines as the one at Everton.

WE'LL SETTLE FOR THREE

● Newcastle United are undoubtedly one of the strongest clubs in the Second League, and there is every probability that they will qualify for the test matches, but that they will prove a match for Aston Villa at Perry Barr is not anticipated by any Midland football enthusiasts for a single moment. Of course the League Champions must not take matters too easily, but, with the Burnley surprise of a few weeks ago and the West Bromwich disaster of Monday last still fresh in their memories, this is hardly likely, and though it is too much to expect the Villa to win by seven goals to one, as they did two seasons ago when the United were last seen at Perry Barr, there ought to be a clear three goals margin between the clubs at the finish.

Saturday 30th January 1897

VILLA 5, NEWCASTLE UTD 0

● Shocking weather prevailed in Birmingham on Saturday, and the ground at Perry Barr was in a fearful state, pools of water lying all over the field. Consequently there were not more than five or six thousand spectators to witness the cup tie between Aston Villa and Newcastle United.

The latter were fully represented, and the Villa had a good team up, only Welford and Reynolds being absent. The Villa kicked off down field, and soon demonstrated they were the cleverer team, though Newcastle played plucky and good football, their right wing frequently making dangerous attacks on the home goal. The ground was against fast and accurate passing, and for a time the Villa forwards shot poorly, Wheldon and Campbell both missing good openings. Ostler dropped the ball right into the Villa goal mouth, but Wilkes, who proved to be in exceptionally good form, effected a clever save. At length, Athersmith, running in brilliant style, quite outpaced the Newcastle backs, and finished a grand individual effort by shooting into the net. The visitors got up, and Collins made a fine centre, but Smellie, a long way off-side, charged Wilkes, and the advantage was neutralised, though immediately afterwards from another splendid run by the Newcastle right, Wilkes was hard pressed to save. Three corners fell to the visitors, and only another good piece of work by Wilkes prevented Connel scoring. Campbell made a nice run and shot, which Watts saved at the expense of a corner, and then the latter, coming out to stop Smith, the ball was passed to Wheldon, who, with a long, dropping shot, put it safely into the net with the two backs right under the bar. Almost immediately Smith scored a third goal from a rebound, and Wheldon added another from a corner. The Villa at half-time led by 4 goals to 0.

The English Cup

The second half requires little description, for the Villa, on the whole, were content to maintain their advantage, and played well within themselves. Newcastle made many clever and determined efforts to score, but were weak in front of goal, and Spencer was playing a wonderfully fine back game. Just before the finish a mis-kick by Stewart put Wheldon on side, and the latter having a clear course, easily tricked Watts and scored the fifth goal, the Villa thus winning by 5 goals to 0.

Newcastle United: Watts; Stewart and White; Ostler, Auld and Stott; Collins, Connel, Smellie, Aitken and Wardrope.

Aston Villa: Wilkes; Spencer and Evans; Chatt, Cowan and Crabtree; Athersmith, Devey, Campbell, Wheldon and Smith.

Saturday 6th February 1897

BURY 0, VILLA 2

● Aston Villa played their return match with Bury at Gigg Lane, before a crowd of 10,000 people. Considering the fearful weather the ground was in capital condition.

Bury kicked off and at once made the pace warm, but Athersmith broke away from a pass by Devey and centred well. Campbell, however, missed the opening, and Wheldon shot wide. Another good run by the Villa forwards was spoiled by a poor shot from Cowan. The Bury left got down cleverly, but Spencer knocked the man off, and Evans cleared, Wheldon at once making a fine run up the left and shooting into Montgomery's

CUP FORECAST

● In past seasons Small Heath have fared badly in the English Cup competition, although they did once succeed in getting into the semi-final, to be defeated by West Bromwich Albion. Last year they were knocked out by Bury, in 1895 by the Albion, and in 1894 by Bolton Wanderers, each game being played at Small Heath, and, curiously enough, in the first round of the competition. Surely they will not allow Notts to follow the example of the other clubs!

There are sure to be a few surprise results tomorrow, but unless there is a tremendous upheaval of form the following clubs should enter the second round of the English Cup competition:-

Aston Villa
Small Heath
Sheffield Wednesday
Blackburn Rovers
Stoke
Liverpool
Bury
Southampton St. Mary's

Millwall Athletic
West Bromwich Albion
Burnley
Newton Heath
Derby County
Everton
Preston North End
Bolton Wanderers

CYCLE TRACK AGREEMENT

● We are in a position to state that arrangements have just been concluded whereby the directors of the Aston Villa Football Club agree to lease to the proprietors of *Sport and Play*, for a term of seven years, the use of the new cycling track they are laying down at the Aston Lower Grounds, for the purpose of promoting cycling and athletic gatherings. There can be no question the directors have taken the right course in this matter, for the *Sport and Play* authorities have had great experience in the management of cycle meetings. They will, as heretofore, 'run' these meetings during the season – at Easter, Whitsuntide, and August Bank Holidays. The League match, Aston Villa v Wolverhampton Wanderers, will be included in the programme for next Easter Monday, and it is also hoped to arrange a big race between Tom Linton and J. Michael, two of the most famous cycling 'professors' of the day. Profiting by the revived interest in professional pedestrianism, too, we understand that an athletic festival will be arranged during the summer to include several professional handicaps in which the League players are expected to take part.

...BUT FIVE WILL DO

● Aston Villa easily accounted for Newcastle United at Perry Barr last week, and those folks who had been expecting to see a close contest were sadly disappointed, for there was practically only one team in it after the first quarter of an hour's play, and the Birmingham club thoroughly deserved their big victory. The ground was in a wretched condition, and it would not have been at all surprising had the referee ordered the game to be postponed, for the meadow was more suitable for mudlarking than for first-class football.

DENNY CAN STILL DAZZLE

● Once again have Small Heath bid good-bye to the English Cup in the first round of the competition, although it was not without a severe struggle that they were ousted by Notts County. Those people who have been declaring that Dennis Hodgetts' footballing days are over, and that Small

hands. Still pressing, Devey forced a corner, but the ball was put behind. Settle and Wyllie ran up nicely, but the latter's shot was very wide. The game continued fast, both ends being visited in turn. A grand piece of play by Crabtree ended in his putting the ball over the bar, and then Athersmith shot outside. Another brilliant run and shot by Wheldon just under the bar was only saved at the expense of a corner. Nothing came of it, and a like result attended another which followed. A beautiful run and centre by Athersmith went to Devey, who skimmed the bar. Crabtree was fouled for holding Settle, but Evans cleared splendidly with his head, and Millar shot yards wide. Athersmith again got off nicely and centred well, but there was not enough steam behind Wheldon's shot, and Montgomery had no difficulty in clearing. The Bury goalkeeper immediately afterwards was lucky in clearing a beautiful shot from Smith, and though a perfect bombardment was kept up on the home goal it escaped. Soon afterwards, however, a magnificent shot by Campbell was only half stopped by Montgomery, and it rolled into the net. Within a couple of minutes, Athersmith ran up the wing and centred beautifully, Wheldon turning the ball over to Campbell, who shot a second goal. Bury got a foul, but Darroch put it into the net without touching anyone, and though a foul followed close in the ball was put behind. Millar put in a lovely shot, which was brilliantly saved by Wilkes throwing himself full length. Nothing more was done, and at the interval the Villa led by 2 goals to 0.

Johnny Campbell

On resuming, Bury at once forced a corner, but the ball was put out. Villa then attacked, and Cowan just missed with a long shot, whilst at the other end Wyllie, when clean off-side, shot into the net, the point being promptly disallowed. Athersmith made a fine run but shot wide, after which he put the ball into Montgomery's hands, Wheldon trying in vain to rush the goalkeeper. Bury played up pluckily and forced a corner, but after an exciting scrimmage the ball was put out. 'Hands' gave them another chance, but it was not utilised, though Millar hit the bar with a capital effort. The Villa were playing well within themselves, and eventually won by 2 goals to 0.

Bury: Montgomery; Darroch and Barbour; Pray, Hendry and Ross; Settle, Wyllie, Millar, Henderson and Plant.

Aston Villa: Wilkes; Spencer and Evans; Chatt, Cowan and Crabtree; Athersmith, Devey, Campbell, Wheldon and Smith.

● Played yesterday at Turf Moor, Burnley, before 4,000 spectators. This was the fixture abandoned in December, owing to bad weather, and yesterday, in the first half, the home team had to face the incline.

The ground was in bad condition, but the Villa at once went to the Burnley end, Athersmith thrice centring after fine runs. The third time Wheldon headed the ball into the net, but the goal was disallowed for obstructing the goalkeeper. However, just after this Campbell scored with a long shot, and the Villa again pressed from the kick-off, Devey sending in a shot which Tatham touched but could not prevent turning into the net. Crabtree sent a good pass to Athersmith, who centred well, and Wheldon headed the wrong side of the post. Burnley then dashed off, and Robertson all but beat Wilkes, but the Villa custodian saved brilliantly. However, the ball was soon transferred to the other end, and again Athersmith centred, and Devey meeting ball, with excellent judgement, he put it through the goal. The Villa were having pretty well all the play, but at length Burnley went away, and after a hot attack Robertson scored their first point.

Heath made a big mistake when they signed him up, were doubtless rather surprised at the display given by the veteran international on Saturday against Notts County. He was by far the cleverest player on the field and it was certainly not his fault that the Heathens failed to enter the second round.

DIARY DATES

● After playing Bury tomorrow, the Villa will not return to Birmingham, but will spend Saturday night and Sunday at Manchester, going on to Burnley on Monday morning.

For winning their English Cup ties on Saturday, the Albion and the Villa players each receive one of Davenport's Pocket Diaries, which will doubtless prove very useful to them. The Small Heath players were offered the same inducement to win, but could not quite manage it.

12 FEBRUARY 1897

THE ACHIEVEMENTS OF ASTON VILLA

● The Villa Committee, though they don't undervalue praise as an incentive to exertion, have, like the management of the Gaiety music hall, more reliance on 'the power of gold.' "Show them what you can do," is all very well, but "We'll give you £5 if you win" is far better, and, having this promise before they went to Lancashire, it was no wonder the men excelled themselves, brought back the full number of points, and made their position at the head of the League practically unassailable. Bury are not a team to be despised at any time, and as they won their cup tie with Stockton by twelve goals to one, their supporters were confident that they could repeat last season's performance and take two points out of the Villa, but the vanity of such hopes was soon seen. The Villa forwards, barring a little uncertainty in shooting, were at their best, and Bury, though they managed to keep the scoring low, were powerless to compete with Athersmith's speed, and Campbell's rushes. The latter, on this season's form, is the best centre-forward in the League, and on Saturday he won unstinted praise from the Bury crowd for his untiring and resourceful work. Smith didn't shine so well as his companions, but it should be remembered that he hasn't the help now he once had. Wheldon is a fine forward, but he prefers to rely on his own efforts, instead of making openings for his partner, as Hodgetts did.

IT'S LOOKING GOOD

The Perry Pets – this title will be no longer available when the club move to their new home at the 'Lower' – have now 32 points to their credit, and as five out of their remaining eight League games are to be played at home, there is little fear of either Everton, Preston, or Derby County overtaking them in the competition, however well these clubs may play. Everton's defeat on their own meadow last week caused great disappointment in Liverpool football circles, for it had been hoped that the 'Toffee Merchants' would win the Championship this season, and so make out for disappointments of previous years. It is not to be, however, and if Liverpool people desire to see the League Cup they will have to come to Birmingham.

BRIEFLETS...

☞ *The Aston Villa players receive £2 each if they win their English Cup tie with Notts County tomorrow.*

☞ *The Villa directors mean to put the new English Cup where burglars cannot get at it – when they have won it.*

☞ *Some of Small Heath's supporters considered the club had a good chance of winning the Birmingham Cup this year. Last week's result – Wolves 8, Heathens 2 – put an end to their aspirations.*

Right from the kick-off the home team gained a corner, and after Toman had sent into the goalmouth Robertson rushed up and scored their second goal. Half-time: Villa, 3; Burnley, 2.

The second half opened quietly but Burnley were first to attack. However, the Villa soon changed the scene of operations, and Devey succeeded in putting through goal from a good centre by Smith. The visitors continued to press, and the Burnley goal had many narrow shaves. Half-way through the second half the Villa were driven back, and a nice centre from Place, jun., was put past Wilkes by Black. the result of an interesting game was:- Villa, 4 goals; Burnley, 3.

Aston Villa: Wilkes; Spencer and Evans; Chatt, Cowan and Crabtree; Athersmith, Devey, Campbell, Wheldon and Smith.

Burnley: Tatham; Reynolds and McLintock; Place (sen), Longair and Taylor; Toman, Black, Robertson, Bowes and Place (jun).

ENGLISH CUP • ROUND 2

Saturday 13th February 1897
VILLA 2, NOTTS COUNTY 1

● The fact of Aston Villa and Notts County being the present leaders of the first and second divisions of the League respectively, lent additional attraction to the English Cup-tie between these clubs, and when the teams turned out at Perry Barr there were quite 20,000 spectators present.

Notts had been training at Hazelwood Ferry, a village on the Trent, and were in the pink of condition, but the Villa, who were without Chatt and Welford, had several men suffering from the effects of their recent hard work in Lancashire. Notts won the toss, and played with a strong breeze and the hill in their favour. They quickly made it evident they were going for all they were worth, and they certainly played high-class and plucky football throughout. There was much more dash in them than in the home team, who appeared a trifle stale. Within five minutes of the start they bore down on the home goal, and gained a free kick in a favourable position. This was splendidly placed by Prescott, and the ball glanced into the Villa net off Bull – a disaster which the Perry Barr spectators did not fail to recognise. The Villa began to play with more spirit, Cowan and Reynolds frequently giving the forwards a chance. The Notts goal had two or three narrow escapes, though Toone and Prescott were playing a fine game, and eventually Athersmith getting possession made a pretty run up the right and centred right into goal, Devey met the ball, and turned it over to Wheldon, who headed past Toone amidst loud cheers a quarter of an hour from the start. The game pro-

Fred Wheldon

gressed with varying fortunes, there being little to choose between the rivals until an unfortunate accident happened. Crabtree and Bramley collided in going for the ball, with the result that the latter had his right leg broken just below the knee. It was a pure accident, and quite a misfortune for the visitors, for Bramley was playing a grand game. He was loudly cheered as he was carried off the field smoking a cigarette. For the remainder of the game Notts were a man short, Bull going to the half-back position, but they never gave up heart, and quite won the sympathies of the crowd by their plucky, skilful, and dashing play. Nothing more was scored up to half time, when the score was 1 goal each.

In the second half it was expected the Villa would win comfortably, but so far from this being the case, Notts played with renewed vigour, and made some exceptionally dangerous attacks on the home goal. Langham and Boucher were especially good, whilst of the defence it would be impossible to speak too highly. The home team certainly had the best of the play and repeatedly bombarded the Notts goal for minutes

A CHAT WITH THE VILLA CAPTAIN

LEAGUE AND CUP PROSPECTS.

● John Devey, captain of the Aston Villa Club, was confined to the house when I paid him a visit yesterday. The large front muscle of his right leg had been 'tapped' in a match recently, he playfully said, and his leg was swathed in bandages, undergoing a sore of medical pickle in order to get it right for today's match.

"Do you think you will win the League Championship?"

"Well, we stand in a very fine position, indeed, and I think we shall come out on top. But, then, you know you can never tell what is going to happen. Just luck at us, for instance. At Christmas we were four points in front, and then we go and lose a couple of matches straight away! And it might happen again. Oh, yes, I think we shall get the cup again."

"And how many points do you think will win the League, anyway?"

"I should think 42. I have an idea that in the eight matches we have yet to play we ought to make 14 points, so that if we only drop four points it will be a very good performance. That would bring us up to 44 points. But, even if we lose six points, I think we shall win. You see we are looking at the safe side. Yes; you are quite right. When you consider that we have only had fifteen first-class men to rely upon and have three or four laid up for the past month practically, we have not done badly."

"Are you going to win tomorrow and finally land the English Cup?"

"Yes; I think we shall beat Notts County, but none of us are holding them too light. You see, the County are an unknown quantity to us, but what is certain to us is they must be a good lot of players. Cup-ties always bring a lot of anxiety, because there is only one chance. It is not like a series of matches in which in a measure you can gain that which you have lost. Well, I don't see why we should not bring off the double event, in winning the League trophy and the English Cup. It has been done before and it will be done again – and you know we were very near it in 1893-4. It looks like coming off this season, but we should feel far more confident if we knew

together, but such was the fine defence of Toone, Prescott, and Gibson – ably assisted by Calderhead and his companions – that it was not until the last 10 minutes that the Villa scored the winning goal, Campbell pushing the ball through from a corner. The Villa thus won by 2 goals to 1.

Notts County: Toone; Prescott and Gibson; Bramley, Calderhead and Crone; Langham, Allan, Boucher, Murphy and Bull.

Aston Villa: Wilkes; Spencer and Evans; Reynolds, Cowan and Crabtree; Athersmith, Devey, Campbell, Wheldon and Smith.

LEAGUE DIVISION ONE

Monday 22nd February 1897

VILLA 3, PRESTON NORTH END 1

● This League match was played yesterday at Perry Barr in beautiful weather. The fact that the two clubs meet next Saturday at Preston in the English Cup drew a big crowd, there being quite 14,000 persons present.

A strong breeze was blowing across the field, and the visitors won the toss. From the kick off Preston got away, and Spencer missing, Boyd was left in a fine position for a shot, but Wilkes cleverly cleared. Again the Preston left came with a dash, Stevenson being only just knocked off the ball as Cowan cleared. A nice run by Smith was followed by a good centre, but Cowan shot wide, and then Preston came down the right, Stevenson being left with the goal at his mercy, but only to shoot over the bar. Athersmith forced a corner, the ball being put behind, but directly afterwards Smith shot into Trainer's hands. The game continued to be very fast, the Villa having slightly the best of the exchanges for a time, though the wind and sun were helping the other side. After Wilkes had cleared a shot at long range Devey and Campbell got away

P.P.

'Proud Preston'

nicely, and passed to Athersmith, whose centre went behind. Still pressing, the Villa left came nicely, a beautiful piece of play by Wheldon and Smith ending in the latter getting the ball across for Devey to meet and cleverly steer into the net after 12 minutes' play. Smith, who was in rare form, made another nice run, and forced a corner, but the ball was put behind. Coming again, Devey crossed to Athersmith, who sent in a terrific shot, Trainer being lucky to clear at the expense of an unproductive corner. Preston got down the right, but only succeeded in driving the ball over. Athersmith made a grand run, and Wheldon shot into Trainer's hands, he being lucky to get it away after dropping it. The Preston goal had further escapes from a fierce bombardment, and at the other end Smith headed just outside from a free kick. Athersmith gained a corner from Dunn but again the ball was put out. The Preston goal escaped in miraculous manner from shots by Reynolds and Wheldon, following on a foul. Crabtree cleverly stopped a dangerous centre, but a corner followed, which was easily got away by Devey, though directly afterwards, from some dashing play, Ecclestone shot just over the Villa bar. Some exciting play followed and Smith initiated a beautiful run, which was spoiled by Devey getting off-side, whilst a moment later Campbell shot wide. At the other end Crabtree twice stopped dangerous attacks in workmanlike fashion, whilst a corner was taken without effect. Trainer twice saved finely from capital shots by Smith, and from a brilliant piece of play by Smith, Wheldon and Athersmith, Campbell, standing right in front, shot just the wrong side of the post. From a foul the Preston goal had the narrowest of escapes, whilst a moment later Wheldon shot wide, and then headed over the bar. Not to be denied, however, Athersmith made another brilliant run and centre and this time Devey headed safely into the net, the interval arriving with the Villa leading by 2 goals to 0.

On resuming, a foul against Athersmith gave Preston an opening, and after an exciting piece of work that all our men were well and strong. If we get through the next two or three weeks all right, and get the men fit again, I think we have a splendid chance. You see, we are in a serious position now, for not only have we got good men injured, but we have not got good men to put in their places. As you readily understand, an accident means a lot to us. No, I am not a very great believer in having too many first-class men in reserve."

"That may be, but the second team might have men of better calibre in it to fall back upon in times of necessity," I ventured.

"Just so. The Villa Committee have been trying to encourage local talent, but it appears that there has not been any good material to work upon, and it maybe that there has been a slight lack of judgement in judging the quality of the men. The result has been that we have done away with a lot of Scottish players verging on first-class, and who frequently lifted the club out of difficulties. On the face of it this playing of local men in the reserve team has been a failure, for we have not found a man within streets of the standard required for the first team."

I ventured to suggest international matters but Devey would not say much about the actions of the Selection Committee of the Football Association.

"What I can say, however," he remarked, "is that I am never at my best in a trial match, like the England and Ireland game. I have noticed when playing against Ireland that there has always been a tendency among the Englishmen to think about their Scottish caps, and the result has been that in the forwards they have played in pairs instead of combining as a line. Two men think that if they play together and into each other's hands they will stand a good chance of being chosen for the game against Scotland, and the centre is left alone to an extent which of necessity makes the whole line suffer. In the inter-League matches, on the other hand, I have always been a success. I have played in four out of the five games, and I should have played in the odd one, only that after selection I was indisposed." – And there is a great deal more than meets the eye in what the Villa captain says about men playing for their individual interests more than for the interests of their side – "And what do you think the success of the Villa team is due to?"

"Ah, I am glad you asked me that. Without doubt it is the good fellowship and the unselfishness which characterise all the men. There is not a man in the team who has the slightest animosity or jealousy against another. I don't care what club it is, whether it is the finest combination of players ever got together, but you can't have success if the very best of feeling does not exist between the men. That is the secret of the Villa's success. I have never been associated with a better lot of players. I hope the Villa club will always get such a class of man. When the standard drops from what it is now, then the trouble will begin."

the ball was headed over the bar. Smith and Crabtree quickly brought the ball down, but the Preston left ran up, and Spencer kicking in front of his own goal, Ecclestone had no difficulty in shooting into the net. Immediately afterwards the Preston goal had the luckiest of escapes from Campbell, the ball rebounding off Trainer as he lay on the ground. The Villa were very wild for a time, and Sanders shot into Wilkes's hands, whilst a corner followed. At length the home team got down, but Smith spoiled a good run by a bad centre. Then Devey, working a nice opening, shot over the bar, and Campbell, with a long one, only just missed the post. A grand run and centre by Athersmith was met by Campbell, who shot hard into Trainer's hands, and two useful fouls to the Villa were allowed to

Charlie Athersmith

pass without further advantage. A corner, however, followed, and Athersmith got the ball into the net, after it had struck the bar. Still pressing, the Villa got another corner, Devey shooting over the bar, and Wheldon being badly tripped right in front, a penalty should have followed, but the referee only allowed an ordinary foul, which was easily cleared. Evans stopped Stevenson when he was dangerous, but Preston came again, and from a strong attack Boyd hit the bar, Crabtree effecting a clever save. The visitors were by no means done with, and made desperate efforts to get on terms, but the Villa defence was safe, and a capital game ended: – Aston Villa, 3 goals; Preston North End, 1.

Preston North End: Trainer; Holmes and Dunn; Blyth, Sanders and Orr; Smith, Ecclestone, Stevenson, Boyd and Henderson.

Aston Villa: Wilkes; Spencer and Evans; Reynolds, Cowan and Crabtree; Athersmith, Devey, Campbell, Wheldon and Smith.

ENGLISH CUP ROUND 3
Saturday 27th February 1897
PRESTON NORTH END 1, VILLA 1

● The tie between these two famous cup fighters was played on the Preston ground, Deepdale, in fine weather, and before a crowd of about 14,000 spectators, extra prices being charged for admission. Both sides were as announced, and appeared in the pink of condition, the Villa having trained during the week at Blackpool.

The visitors lost the toss and kicked off against the wind and sun. Preston were the first to attack, but they only drove the ball out, and the Villa rushing down, Campbell got in a good shot which cannoned off the legs of one of the backs. Devey made a good run, and after some pretty play by Reynolds, Campbell, Devey, and Athersmith, the latter put in a beautiful shot which Trainer only saved at the expense of a corner. The ball was well placed, and Athersmith drove it into the net, the goal, however, being promptly disallowed for some infringement which was not observable in the press seats. Both sides attacked in turn, the pace being very hot, and the Prestonians certainly having the best of the exchanges. They were keener on the ball than the Villa, whose combination was frequently broken up by the resolute play of the home half-backs. Sanders and Orr especially. The last-named got in a fine shot which only just missed the posts, and Preston attacked strongly, forcing several unproductive corners and getting a big advantage from fouls by Reynolds and Cowan. The Villa broke away, and Wheldon sent in a long shot which hit the side net. Stevenson got a good opening but shot wide, and then Reynolds was twice penalised for using his hands, a corner following upon the latter which was so cleverly placed that the ball was scrimmaged into the Villa net, the first goal falling to Preston amidst tumultuous cheering 31 minutes after the start. The Villa made strenuous attempts to get on terms, but were well held in check, Preston

TOUGH TASK AT DEEPDALE

● Will Aston Villa survive the third round of the English Cup competition? That is the one topic of conversation among football enthusiasts in this district at the present time, and opinion on the matter appears to be pretty evenly divided. Preston North End are a great team this season, and on their own ground are practically invincible; their eleven is strong all round, and their position in the League table is proof that they are a team of which their supporters may well be proud. Still, no club have played in better form away from home than have the Villa, and when it is remembered that the only clubs against whom the Birmingham men have suffered defeat on foreign soil this season are Sunderland and West Bromwich Albion, whereas they have brought off victories at Everton, Bury, Burnley, Blackburn, Derby, Sheffield, and Wolverhampton, it will be recognised that the Villa's chances of winning at Deepdale tomorrow week are by no means hopeless.

INTRODUCING JACK

● After several weeks' absence on account of illness, Jack Reynolds made a welcome reappearance in the home ranks, and once again played a capital game. Reynolds was born at Blackburn on February 21st, 1870, so that he attains his twenty-seventh birthday on Sunday next. Ten years ago he enlisted in the army, joining the East Lancashire Regiment, which was then stationed at Belfast, and there it was that his footballing abilities were first recognised. At that time he was playing at centre half-back, and he captained the regimental team with credit both to himself and the army. In 1889 the Belfast Distillery Club bought him out of the army, and he played for them during that season, aiding them to win the Irish Association Cup, and being chosen to play for Ireland in the international games with

JOHN REYNOLDS

England, Scotland, and Wales. The following year he joined the Ulster club, and again had the honour of playing in three international games. His form against England at Wolverhampton was so good that he received a magnificent offer from West Bromwich Albion, which he accepted, and materially assisted that club to win the English Cup, when Aston Villa were so unexpectedly beaten in the final tie in 1892. The English Association had now discovered that Reynolds was an Englishman by birth, and straightway 'capped' him against both Scotland and Wales. After two years with the 'Throstles' he was induced to throw in his lot with the Villa, and it is quite needless to remind Birmingham people of the excellent work which he has done for the League Champions. Reynolds possesses no fewer than twelve international caps, while he has also been selected to play for the English League on several occasions.

INTERNATIONAL VILLA

● The Villa team on Saturday included no less than seven international players, viz., Reynolds, Cowan, Crabtree, Athersmith, Devey, Campbell, and Smith, while an eighth name might also be added in Wheldon, for the ex-Heathen will be doing duty for England against Ireland at Nottingham tomorrow. Yet, without these 'stars' playing, they could only manage to defeat a Second Division League club, who for over half the game had only ten men, by a goal, even though the game was played on their own meadow. Not a very brilliant performance!

having the best of matters to the interval, when they led by 1 goal to nil.

On resuming the Villa quickly settled down to play better football than in the first half, and within five minutes they drew level, Campbell scoring a beautiful goal from grand play by Athersmith and Smith. Wilkes had to run out and clear a long pass from Boyd, and when Campbell was well placed at the other end "hands" pulled him up. Preston repeatedly made dangerous incursions into the Villa quarters, but Spencer and Evans were quite reliable, and were well helped by the halves. Athersmith and Devey repeatedly beat Orr and Dunn, but Holmes was in great form, and Trainer kept goal splendidly. As time drew near the pace slackened somewhat, but Preston played desperately to the finish without getting anything tangible. Just before the close the Villa made a fine run, and Cowan sent in a lovely, curly shot, which Trainer saved in miraculous fashion just as it was going into the corner of the net. Nothing more was done, and an exciting game ended in a draw of one goal each.

Preston North End: Trainer; Holmes and Dunn; Blyth, Sanders and Orr; Smith, Pratt, Stevenson, Boyd and Henderson.

Aston Villa: Wilkes; Spencer and Evans; Reynolds, Cowan and Crabtree; Athersmith, Devey, Campbell, Wheldon and Smith.

ENGLISH CUP ROUND 3 REPLAY

Wednesday 3rd March 1897
VILLA 0, PRESTON NORTH END 0

● The undecided tie between Aston Villa and Preston North End was replayed yesterday at Perry Barr. The weather was very cold and boisterous, but fine, and there was an attendance of about 12,000 persons. Except that Tait played in place of Holmes in the Preston team the sides were the same as on Saturday.

Preston won the toss, and took advantage of the wind. From the kick-off uphill the Villa at once got away on the right, but though Athersmith got in a beautiful centre Smith shot yards wide. Still having the best of it, a lovely piece of work by Wheldon put Campbell in a good position, but he also was outside the mark. Evans cleverly stopped the Preston right, and again a little later he did a grand piece of work. The Villa forwards made a splendid run, but though their passing was of the finest description Trainer got in a fine save. Another beautiful run and centre by Smith was only saved by Trainer at the expense of a corner. Nothing came of it, and when the Preston left got away they were pulled up in clever fashion by Spencer, who was showing grand defence. Athersmith and Devey ran smartly, and the former dropped the ball just over the bar, whilst Reynolds shot out after a strong and determined attack had threatened serious danger to the visitors. At this period of the game the Villa were having considerably the best of the play, but though their midfield work was so fine, the Preston defence prevented them getting any tangible advantage, half-backs, backs, and goalkeeper all being at their best. Sanders was particularly prominent with clever head work and persistent play, being always on the ball, whilst the kicking and tackling of Preston's backs was of the best order. Try as they would, the Villa could not get the ball into the net, Wheldon shooting over the bar, and Crabtree heading just past the corner of the goal. Trainer twice repelled dangerous shots in clever style, and then Campbell headed over from a corner. A foul against the visitors gave the Villa a nice opening, but nothing resulted, the visiting goal having an extremely narrow escape, whilst a moment later a corner taken by the Villa was safely negotiated. Preston at length broke away, and made things lively for a time, but the home defence was equal to the occasion, Evans and Spencer both playing finely with excellent support from Crabtree, Cowan, and Reynolds. A fine run and shot from Devey and Athersmith was cleared by Trainer, and then Boyd, with a capital opening, shot over the Villa bar. Wheldon put the ball into Trainer's

ENGLAND CALL FOR ATHERSMITH

● In addition to Wheldon, another Aston Villa forward will be assisting the 'old country' against the pick of the Emerald Isle tomorrow, Athersmith having been chosen to play in consequence of the inability of Bassett to turn out. Should the local representatives give a good account of themselves in this contest, there is every likelihood that they will be 'capped' against Scotland in April, and then there will be a trio of Villa players in the team, for Crabtree can be regarded as a certainty.

A FEW QUERIES

● Will The Aston Lower Grounds be ready for the Villa to play their return League match with Liverpool on the 13th?

● Are Aston Villa going to bring off the 'double event' – the League Championship and the English Cup – this season?

● How many representatives are the Argus supposed to send to Perry Barr to report the Villa matches?

● Are the Aston Villa committee looking out for a new back?

● Is Welford going to play again this season?

● How many of the Villa players will get their international caps this year?

● Are the Villa committee sorry that they did not avail themselves of the opportunity to secure Boucher, the Notts County centre-forward, when he offered himself to them a couple of seasons ago?

PREPARED

● Yesterday the Aston Villa football team left Birmingham for Holt Fleet, where, under the superintendence of Mr. J. Lees and the trainer, Grierson, they will be subjected to a little quiet training, in view of the two heavy matches against Preston North End next week – the League match at Perry Barr, on Monday, and the English Cup-tie on the following Saturday at Preston. After the League match, the men will be taken to Blackpool, where they will finish their preparation for the Cup-tie.

WEDDING GIFT FOR ARTHUR

● There was an interesting gathering of representative Birmingham and District footballers at the Colonnade last evening, when a number of presentations were made to Mr Arthur V. Cooknell in recognition of his unfailing courtesy and energy as hon. secretary of the Birmingham and District Football League since its institution. Mr I. Whitehouse, the president of the League, was in the chair, and amongst those supporting him were Mr C. Crump (president of the Birmingham and District Counties' Association), Mr J. Adams, Mr J. O. Orr, Mr G. B. Ramsay, Mr W. H. Rinder, Mr C. Crump, jun., Mr J. Round, Mr A. Jones, Mr J. McKnight, &c. the presentations consisted of a handsome silver inkstand, suitably inscribed, an illuminated address, and a purse containing £24, subscribed to by all the clubs in the League, the Management Committee, and the referees on the occasion of Mr Cooknell's marriage. Complimentary speeches were made by the Chairman, Mr Crump, Mr J. Adams, &c, and Mr Cooknell made a happy response. A capital smoking concert followed.

hands, and at the other end Evans got rid of a corner forced by Blyth and Sanders, the interval arriving with no goals on either side.

On resuming, a splendid run and centre by Athersmith was the first incident of note, but Trainer threw out the ball from the corner of the goal in the grandest fashion. Smith then led an attack on the other wing, but when getting dangerous over-ran the ball, and Tait got it away. Still pressing, Devey sent in a terrific shot, which struck the stay-post of the net – but outside the goal – and though the Villa returned to the attack it was without avail, the Preston defence being fine in the extreme. Breaking away on the left Henderson tried a

Steve Smith

long shot which Wilkes had plenty of time to deal with, and then, coming down again, Devey shot wide and Campbell put a long shot the wrong side of the post. Dunn was forced to concede a corner, but Stevenson headed the ball out of danger, and, running smartly up the field, did a good piece of work, only, however, to be knocked off the ball by Evans at the critical moment. A corner followed to the visitors, but it was easily dealt with, and a strong attack by the Villa was beaten off, Trainer saving cleverly from Athersmith and Campbell heading over the centre of the bar. After Devey had shot wide, Trainer brought off another brilliant save from a well-placed corner, whilst Wheldon was knocked off the ball when favourably placed, and though another corner followed it was got away. Preston made several breaks away, but the Villa defence was very safe, and there was little danger with them. A magnificent save by Trainer from a grand shot by Campbell was loudly cheered, and then Athersmith with a beauty hit the post, and a little later the cross-bar. Orr hit the Villa post with a long cross-shot, and though the Villa forced two corners and generally had the best of the exchanges, they could not get the ball past Trainer, a splendidly contested match, in which both sides played the finest football, ending in a pointless draw.

Preston North End: Trainer; Tait and Dunn; Blyth, Sanders and Orr; Smith, Pratt, Stevenson, Boyd and Henderson.

Aston Villa: Wilkes; Spencer and Evans; Reynolds, Cowan and Crabtree; Athersmith, Devey, Campbell, Wheldon and Smith.

LEAGUE DIVISION ONE
Saturday 6th March
NOTTINGHAM FOREST 2, VILLA 4

● There was a capital attendance at the Town Ground, where these teams met in the return League match, both sides being representative.

The Villa lost the toss, and kicked off, Athersmith at once forcing a corner, from which Reynolds all but scored. McInnes made a fine run, but was pulled up by Spencer, and the Villa right going up, Campbell shot wide. Cowan stopped the Forest left, and Athersmith and Devey made a couple of fine runs, the Villa attacking strongly. A foul against the home team gave the visitors a chance, and the ball being beautifully placed by Crabtree, Devey headed the first goal, 14 minutes from the start. The Forest, aided by the wind, forced the pace. Adrian Capes and McInnes both being prominent, though their work in front of goal was scarcely satisfactory. At the other end Allsopp was lucky in stopping a shot from Campbell, but just afterwards he cleverly threw out from a 'header' by Athersmith, which dropped just short of the bar. For a time the Forest had the best of matters, and made things very warm round the Villa goal, but the visiting defence was splendid, Crabtree, Cowan, and Reynolds al lending grand assistance to the backs. The Villa got a couple of corners, but they were unproductive, whilst other shots were cleared by the home backs. McInnes tried hard to get in, but, though allowed

ASTON VILLA RESERVE V BOURNBROOK

● Bournbrook had a visit from the 'Junior Villans' on Saturday. There was splendid football weather and a big gate. The visitors brought a strong combination, including John Cowan and Whitehouse. Newman won the toss, and the game opened evenly. the Bourns forced a corner, which came to nothing, and after 20 minutes' play the Villa scored the first goal by a fine cross shot which Coates made no effort to stop. Shortly after from a throw-in near goal Cowan scored a second. The Bourns although two behind played pluckily, and had the hardest lines in not scoring. Newman forced Whitehouse over the line, but the referee ruled that the ball did not go over. Still attacking Edwards shot clean into the net. The whistle had gone for outside just before so this also was disallowed. Just before half-time Keeling hit the upright with a terrific shot. Half-time: Villa 2, Bournbrook, 0. In the second half the home team seemed to play more accurately against the wind and gave Whitehouse and his backs not a little

JOHN COWAN

work to do. It was very evident the visiting team were a little surprised at finding such strong opposition, and tried their utmost to increase their lead. Coates stopped several beautiful shots. About half way through Bournbrook scored and then put in all they knew to draw level. Two minutes before time Keeling equalised, amid hearty cheering, and when the whistle blew Bournbrook was again clustering round the Villa goal. Result: Bournbrook, 2 goals; Aston Villa Reserve, 2.

EXCURSIONS TO PRESTON

● Birmingham footballers will be glad to know that Mr. W. McGregor has arranged with the London and North-Western Railway Company to run special half-day excursions to Preston next Saturday for the English Cup-tie between Aston Villa and Preston North End. The first train will leave New Street at 11.20 a.m., and is due at Deepdale (adjoining the ground) in plenty of time for the kick-off. The fare is only 4s.

BRIEFLET

☞ *Immediately after their League match with Preston at Perry Barr this afternoon, the Villa will leave for Blackpool, where they will complete their training for next Saturday's Cup-tie. They have been at Holt Fleet since Wednesday.*

UNDER LOCK AND KEY

● Hail, Aston Villa, Champions of the League for 1896-97! By their signal victory over Preston on Monday the Villa have made their position at the head of the League quite secure, and the much-prized trophy held in connection with the competition will remain within our midst for another twelve months at least. Although the Birmingham club have won the Championship on two previous occasions, there are quite fifty per cent. of their supporters who have never had so much as a glimpse of the Cup. Were not the Art Gallery authorities to refuse to allow the trophy to be placed in their keeping, everyone would be able to see it whenever they pleased. As it is, the Villa committee dread a repetition of the English Cup fiasco, and keep the Cup safely under lock and key, only producing it on high days and holidays.

plenty of rope by Reynolds, he found Spencer too good for him, and the interval arrived with the Villa leading by 1 goal to 0.

Charlie Athersmith

The start of the second half was sensational. From a nice piece of play by McInnes, Spencer (Forest right) drew level with a pretty oblique shot, but the Villa at once went up, a brilliant run by Campbell, Devey, and Athersmith ending in John Cowan scoring a beautiful goal. Almost immediately the Forest left again got away, and Evans heading the ball on to Spencer (Forest), the latter returned it into the net amidst enthusiastic cheers. This, however, was only the signal for another effort by the Villa, and after some more pretty play Devey again put the visitors ahead from a foul. Four goals within 17 minutes was pretty warm work, and the pace seemed to tell on the Forest, who 'cracked up' from this point. The Villa went strongly to the finish. Wheldon adding another goal with a remarkable overhead screw shot, and narrowly missing another. The Villa thus won by 4 goals to 2.

Notts Forest: Allsopp; Scott and Iremonger; Stewart, Frank Forman and Wragg; Spencer, Adrian Capes, Richards, Arthur Capes and McInnes.

Aston Villa: Wilke; Spencer and Evans; Reynolds, James Cowan and Crabtree; Athersmith, Devey, Campbell, Wheldon and John Cowan.

ENGLISH CUP • ROUND 3 • 2ND REPLAY
Wednesday 10th March 1897
PRESTON NORTH END 2, VILLA 3

● For the third time of asking these clubs met yesterday at Bramall Lane Ground, Sheffield, in the third round of the English Cup. Fortunately the weather proved fine, and there was an immense attendance of spectators, quite 22,000 persons being present. The teams were as advertised, the only change from the previous matches being the reappearance of Holmes in the Preston back division, and the substitution of John Cowan for Smith on the Villa outside left.

There was very little breeze blowing, but winning the toss the Villa took what advantage there was to be gained from it. From a kick-off a foul enabled Evans to put the ball in the mouth of the Preston goal, a corner resulting, which was safely negotiated, though the ball was not far wide when it went outside. A strong attack was maintained by the Villa, but the ball was eventually got away, Smith sprinting down the wing, but only to kick out, Crabtree in attendance all the way. The Preston left forced an unproductive corner from Reynolds, but some capital defence was shown by the Birmingham team, Evans doing some useful work. A foul against Cowan in mid-field was profitless, and then the scene of operations was changed, a beautiful run by Devey and Athersmith ending in the latter dropping the ball into the corner of the goal, but only for

John Devey

Trainer to bring off one of his wonderful saves. Again the Villa attacked, the forwards playing splendidly together, but the Preston defence was grand, both half-backs and backs showing great form. Some good play by Evans put the ball to Athersmith, Cowan, however, being unable to utilise his centre. "Hands" pulled Athersmith up when he had got away easily, and, though the Villa gained a corner Preston cleared in good style. Dunn and Sanders were slightly hurt, but the game proceeded, and the latter was quickly noticeable for some really grand head and footwork. Crabtree and Reynolds on the other side were always on the alert, and were playing in their best form, time after time stopping the opposing forwards and helping their own vanguard to attack. Campbell broke away, but shot wide, and then Preston came down on the left,

BONUS INCENTIVE

● The Villa players have been staying at Blackpool since Tuesday, and should be greatly benefitted thereby. They proceed to Preston tomorrow morning, when the team will be finally chosen, and as the players will receive £3 bonus if they prove victorious, they can be relied upon to put forth their very best efforts. Several excursion trains will be run from Birmingham to Preston, and the Villa will certainly not lack supporters. The prices of admission to the ground have been doubled, and this will doubt-less deter many from patronising the game, for working men are apt to think twice before they part with a shilling to witness a game the like of which can generally be seen for sixpence. With both teams in their best form, the game will be an extremely close one, for the Villa's slight superiority will be neutralised by the fact that the North Enders are playing on their own meadow.

A GAY DAY OUT

● West Bromwich Albion pay a visit to the 'gay Metropolis' tomorrow to oppose the Corinthians, who can be relied upon to win, for the 'Throstles' are never difficult to dispose of when there is nothing at stake.

POT-HUNTING

● The Birmingham Football Association will have to look to it, or their once-coveted pot will fall into contempt. Before the advent of the League, midland footballers looked on it as second only to the English Cup, but from the proceedings of Saturday last there doesn't appear to be any disposition among the competing clubs to make any extraordinary effort to obtain possession of it, and the Association might do worse than give a hint to the committees of certain clubs that it would be more straight-forward to scratch than to send their men on the field not caring a button whether they won or not.

5 MARCH 1897

PERFECT AT PRESTON

● I happened to be one of about a thousand who made the journey to Preston last week in the hope of seeing the Villa defeat North End. For a great wonder, the trains arrived at the advertised time, and the 'Brummagem brigade' were able to get good places before the ground was quite filled. The arrangements for the press were in every way satisfactory, though what would have happened had it rained I tremble to think, for the majority of the reporters present were provided with seats at a table in front of the grand stand, and there would have been no possibility of getting under cover once the game had commenced. However, the weather was delightfully fine, so there was no reason to dwell upon what might have been. The game was fiercely contested throughout, and it cannot be denied that, on the day's play, the Villa were extremely fortunate in escaping with a draw.

NEW SIGNING - ONE

● The Villa have done an excellent stroke of business in securing the trans-fer of Harry Johnston from Sunderland, for they have not been too well off for first-class defenders this season. Originally a member of the Clyde club (Glasgow,) he joined Sunderland in 1894, and was at that time regarded as one of the cleverest left half-backs in the kingdom. This season he has not been able to play in many games, having been laid up with scarlet fever for several months, but he has now completely recovered, and if he is in any-thing like his old form he will prove a decided acquisition to the Villa team.

NEW SIGNING - TWO

● The second new player whom the Villa have secured – Keit, from a

only to be driven back. Some brilliant play was shown by John Cowan and Crabtree, both of whom sent in good shots, whilst Trainer threw out from under the bar from Campbell. A couple of fouls against the Villa looked dangerous, but Wilkes threw out, and Campbell, racing away, he passed to Athersmith, whose centre was too low and easily cleared by Dunn. A pretty run by John Cowan, Wheldon, and Campbell was spoiled by Athersmith getting offside, and a little later Cowan, after making a lovely run, shot wide. Evans was fouled for charging Pratt – though perfectly legitimately – but Blyth put the ball over the bar. Devey, Campbell, and Athersmith got away together in line, and from the latter's centre Campbell headed into goal, Trainer putting the ball over the bar. Nothing came from the corner, but directly afterwards Cowan and Wheldon ran up the left, and the last-named get-ting in a beautiful centre, it was met by Athersmith, who headed the first goal for the Villa, after 38 min-utes' play. The goal was the consummation of a very fine piece of football, and was loudly observed. On resuming, the Villa attacked again, a beautiful passing run by Cowan, Devey, and Campbell ending in the ball being driven out, whilst a moment later Trainer saved in marvellous fashion from a stiff scrimmage in front of the goal. Devey, Athersmith, and Campbell came again, and Dunn was lucky to save from the latter. From a foul against Evans for handling the ball when Smith was close in, Preston made matters warm for the Villa, but the Birmingham defence was sound. Crabtree doing some fine work in goal along with James Cowan and the backs. The ball had just been driven over the Preston line when half-time was called, the Villa leading by 1 goal to 0.

Restarting, Athersmith at once ran up the right, and a foul against Sanders from his centre put the Villa in a good position. A corner followed, but the ball was easily got away, only for John Cowan to come again and get in a splendid centre, which Trainer cleared with difficulty. Campbell putting the ball under the bar, but Trainer threw out, and nothing came from a corner forced by Campbell and Cowan. Not to be denied, however, the Villa attacked strongly, and a brilliant piece of play by Athersmith and Devey ended in

Fred Wheldon

Campbell scoring a pretty goal. Some sensational play followed, for no sooner had the game been restarted than from a foul in midfield Holmes dropped the ball well in front, and it glanced through the Villa posts off someone's head. It was a lucky goal, but it put new life into the Prestonians, and for a time they showed great dash. Both sides seemed excited by the turn events had taken, and the play was wild, but the Villa soon settled down again, and showed fine football. From grand runs by Devey and Athersmith, the Preston goal had two marvellous escapes. Hands against Cowan put Preston on the attack, but the Villa defence was wonderfully sound. Spencer and Crabtree greatly distinguishing themselves. Pratt headed over from a corner, and then the Preston goal had a lucky escape from the Villa left, Trainer throwing himself full length on the ground, and just keeping the ball out. Athersmith returned it, but John Cowan shot over the bar. Stevenson was knocked off the ball when in a good position, and though some exciting work followed in front of the Villa posts, the defence was too good, and nothing resulted. Stevenson stopped a very dangerous attack by the Villa, but John Cowan steered the ball into the Preston net from a foul, only to be given off-side. Directly afterwards, in another hot fusillade, Wheldon shot, and when Trainer threw out John Cowan returned the ball, Wheldon rolling both it and Trainer into the net. Again the referee disallowed the point on the plea of interfering with the goalkeeper; but not to be denied, Cowan and Wheldon got the ball well across, and Athersmith headed the third goal. Both sides were showing signs of the hard work, though the Villa were going the stronger of the two, and held their opponents well in hand, their three half-backs doing splendid work. Just when the game seemed all over another foul enabled Holmes to drop the ball into goal, junior Glasgow club, – is an inside left forward of great promise, and though he is not yet clever enough for a position in the League eleven he will have plenty of opportunities to develop his powers in the reserve team, for whom he will probably make his first appearance tomorrow against Brierley Hill Alliance at Perry Barr.

NEW SIGNING - THREE

● Yet another new man has been booked, although he will not come to Birmingham until next season. Barr, who has been playing at full back for Third Lanark in their Scottish Cup ties, is the player, and if he is as good as the Scotch papers say, the Villa will have done well to get his signature attached to a League form.

LOCAL LADS MAKE GOOD

● Some people are never satisfied. One would imagine that Aston Villa supporters, at any rate, had little to complain of, seeing that their club are almost certain to gain the League Championship for the second season in succession, while they also possess an excellent chance of winning the English Cup. But there are malcontents even among them, and their grievance appears to be that the Villa committee do not encourage local talent as they should do, and that Scotch players always have preference over English ones. What utter nonsense this is! The first team, which is composed of six local players and five 'importations' (of whom only two have been brought from Scotland,) have proved themselves to be the best eleven in the country this season. Now let us look at the other side of the picture. The reserve team, in which the local players are able to show off their abilities, hold a very poor position in the Birmingham League table, even if they finish among the first half-dozen clubs at the end of the season. For goodness sake let us hear no more about this 'boycotting of local players,' especially as there is not one iota of truth in it.

NOT QUITE UP TO IT

● The game at Preston was far from being equal to many exhibitions the Villa have given this year, and it cannot be denied that their display greatly chagrined their supporters, not so much from the result, for, considering Preston's form, that was satisfactory enough, as because it demonstrated that many of the Villa players are unable to rise to a great occasion, and lose their heads when bustled by energetic opponents.

PASSING GAME NEEDS IMPROVING

● The training the men had undergone had decidedly improved their stamina, and they had need of it all before the match was over, but if they had devoted more of their time to a study of the art of passing, they wouldn't have had to do their work twice over. Athersmith was the best man on the Villa side, which means that he was the best forward on the field. He suffered somewhat from the weakness of his partner, but a little extra work never comes amiss to him, and whenever he got the ball the North End were in danger. Campbell also did well, but Devey and Wheldon seemed to have their hearts in their mouths, and their passing was at times ridiculous. Cowan was easily the best of the half-backs, Crabtree had probably received orders to help Evans and did not back up his forwards so well as usual, while Reynolds, though showing considerable skill, put his side in danger by his trickiness, Spencer was not so good as usual, though Mr Bentley praises his display highly, but Evans improves wonderfully, and Crabtree might, with advantage, trust him more.

BRIEFLET

☞ *The Villa-Preston games have been very acceptable to the club exchequers, both League and Cup-tie gates being pooled and equally divided between the clubs. The League match at Perry Barr a fortnight ago produced £550, the Cup-tie at Preston £867, and the replayed Cup-tie at Perry Barr £548 – total £1,965 – while they have yet another Cup-tie and League match to play.*

Wilkes making a fine save by pushing it over the bar on the top of the net. The corner which followed was well placed, and Preston scored from a scrimmage. From now to the finish the Villa easily held their own, and finally won an interesting and exciting game by 3 goals to 2.

Preston North End: Trainer; Holmes and Dunn; Blyth, Sanders and Orr; Smith, Pratt, Stevenson, Boyd and Henderson.

Aston Villa: Wilkes; Spencer and Evans; Reynolds, James Cowan, and Crabtree; Athersmith, Devey, Campbell, Wheldon and John Cowan.

LEAGUE DIVISION ONE

Saturday 13th March 1897
VILLA 0, LIVERPOOL 0

● Favoured by fine weather, the return League match between these clubs – who meet next Saturday in the semi-final for the English Cup – at Perry Barr, was attended by upwards of 22,000 people. The Villa lost the toss, and played against the wind and hill.

Liverpool were the first to settle down, Allan twice troubling Whitehouse with long shots, the second of which produced a corner. Nothing came of it, however, Spencer getting the ball away. Cowan and Devey made a nice run, and Athersmith got in a good centre, but John Cowan's shot was wide. Some interesting play followed in the centre, Liverpool undoubtedly having the best of it. Spencer, however, was in his most brilliant mood, and permitted no liberties. Liverpool forced two more unproductive corners, though McCartney, Bradshaw, and Allan made matters warm round the Villa posts, and Geary, after a lovely piece of play, shot hard and straight, Whitehouse bringing off an excellent save. Try as they would, the Villa could make no impression on the Liverpool defence, the visitors' half-backs and backs showing grand form, and the whole team being quicker on the ball than the Birmingham brigade. In front of goal, however, the visitors failed completely; Allan once stood with no one to beat but Whitehouse, but he shot yards over the bar. John Cowan was knocked off the ball when about to shoot, but Liverpool had all the best of it up to the interval, though no goals were scored.

On resuming the Villa were the first to attack on the right, but Cowan and Campbell shot over the bar. A corner to them was unproductive, and at this point Crabtree strained the muscles of his thigh, and had to be assisted off the field. The Villa played ten men for the remainder of the game, but – like their opponents in the first half – they had all the best of the play, and the Liverpool goal had some remarkable escapes. Storer, however, kept goal splendidly and made many fine saves. Try as they would, the Villa could not get the ball into the net, though Athersmith hit the side and

Johnny Campbell

dropped it on the top, whilst Devey struck the bar. Once John Cowan sent in a beauty, which completely beat Storer, and, in the opinion of most of those in a position to judge, the ball was well over the line when Dunlop hooked it out, the referee only allowing a corner. The home team pressed continually, barring one or two breaks-away by Bradshaw and Allan, but they could not score, and the game ended in a pointless draw.

Liverpool: Storer; Goldie and Dunlop; McCartney, Neill and Cleghorn; Geary, Michael, Allan, D. Hannah and Bradshaw.

Aston Villa: Whitehouse; Spencer and Evans; Reynolds, James Cowan and Crabtree; Athersmith, Devey, Campbell, Wheldon and John Cowan.

THROUGH AT LAST!

● After three most stubborn contests with Preston North End, in which both sides have shown some of the best football ever seen in a Cup-tie – Aston Villa yesterday asserted their right to enter the semi-final stage of the English Cup competition. Like the predecessors, the game at Bramall Lane was characterised by a skill and resolution not often met with in such matches, and vanquished though they were, Preston North End proved themselves worthy foemen, fought a gallant battle, and only succumbed to a cleverer team in the pink of condition. That the Villa thoroughly deserved their victory was admitted by everyone, and a greater margin than 3 goals to 2 would have been a more accurate index of the way the game went. Besides the three goals scored, the Birmingham men got the ball into the Preston net on two other occasions, and with regard to at least one of them the general opinion was that it should have been allowed. The Preston goals were both rather on the lucky side, though from the splendid way in which they played up it would have been hard lines on them had they not scored.

BAD WEATHER DELAYS MOVE

● A month or two ago it was authoritatively stated that Aston Villa's new home at the Lower Grounds would be opened on March 13th, but the bad weather has prevented the work being got on with as quickly as was expected, and the return League fixture with Liverpool on that date will be fulfilled at Perry Barr.

FIRST TEAM DEMAND

● The Villa committee and Whitehouse, the ex-Grimsby Town goalkeeper, have been at loggerheads of late, the reason being that the '£300 transfer man' objects to play in the reserve team. It is understood that Everton are anxious to secure his services, but the Villa committee are not willing to release him, and Whitehouse will be wise to hide his disappointment, and make the best of matters.

GOOD ENOUGH TO BEAT ANY TEAM

Villa's play at Nottingham was good enough to beat any team, and had they only performed as well against the North End, they would have earned some £700 less than they had done, so that it's perhaps as well, from the directors' point of view, they didn't. Athersmith, who always improves with training, raced away when he liked, and Campbell, who is the finest centre forward in England, played one of his best games. Devey also was good, but Wheldon was poor; training doesn't seem to pull him up as it should do. Crabtree, James Cowan, and Spencer have no superiors in their positions, but Reynolds, being opposed to the fastest and cleverest of the Notts forwards, McInnes, could hardly be expected to shine.

KEEP AN EYE ON KERR

This is the season when the papers daily announce new captures for all the leading football clubs, and on Saturday the Villa trotted out five new men in their second team before a critical crowd. It may be said at once that not one of them is good enough for the first team, and it was plain that some of them never would be, but all of them are young, and it is probable that one or two will develop into good players if they remain with the Villa, Kerr in particular giving one this idea.

● A crowd of about 30,000 people assembled at Bramall Lane on Saturday to witness the semi-final tie between Aston Villa and Liverpool, who the previous week had played a draw in the League. Liverpool were at full strength, Becton re-appearing, but the Villa were without Crabtree, Griffiths, of the Reserve, taking his place. The weather was fine, and the ground in beautiful condition, whilst the breeze was only moderate.

The Villa, losing the toss, kicked off, and at once attacked, but Dunlop and then Goldie cleared. Geary and Michael got away in nice style, but Allan got a long way offside, and was pulled up by the referee before he shot into the net. Athersmith ran and centred well, but Wheldon missed the ball, and Liverpool, attacking on the left, forced an unproductive corner. Allan again got offside, and Neill was fouled for jumping, the Liverpool goal having a very narrow escape. Fouls against Athersmith and James Cowan put the Villa defence under test, Whitehouse making a fine save under the bar. Cowan, Devey, and Wheldon ran and passed well, but the latter's shot at long range was wide of the mark. John Cowan forced a corner, but it came to nothing, and a couple of fouls against Michael shared a similar fate. Campbell tried a long shot, which Storer easily saved, whilst at the other end, Evans missing his kick, Michael stood with the goal open, but kicked over, then Cowan sent in a beauty, which Storer cleverly saved, rolling over with the ball, but getting it away, whilst directly afterwards he brought off another fine block. Liverpool got away on the left, and Bradshaw and Allan forced a corner. this was cleared, and the Villa attacked strongly, but there was no steam behind Campbell's shot. The respective goalkeepers were called on, but Storer was found the most work to do, and was kept busily employed. Reynolds and James Cowan were doing grand work in conjunction with the

THE FOOTBALL CRITICS

Who from September unto May
The call to duty must obey,
And write of football day by day?
The critics.

Who scribble with impartial pen
On football matters, football men
(And guess at what they dinna ken)?
the critics.

Who sit in judgement on a game,
And merits of the teams proclaim,
Or, blaming, signify the same?
The critics.

Who never shout the word "Offside!"
Or rule of referee deride,
But all their partisanship hide?
The critics.

Who nothing e'er extenuate,
Or aught set down in malice? – great
Tenets of the lofty state –
The critics.

Who're very, very wide-awake,
And never – hardly ever make
What men are prone to – a mistake?
The critics.

TRUTH HURTS

● The letter which appeared in Monday's Argus, signed 'An Old Villa Player,' advocating the inclusion of Welford in the team to oppose Liverpool tomorrow has caused quite a stir in local football circles, and everyone has been wondering who was the author of it. That it was a sensible letter everyone who read it will admit, but, all the same, it is doubtful if the editor would have published it had he known from whom it came. It appears that a few boys attending one of the local grammar schools take a great interest in the Argus correspondence column, and one of these – who has not yet reached the age of fifteen – was responsible for the effusion.

Had the youngster attached his own name to the communication, it would probably have been passed over without comment, but because he signed it, 'An Old Villa Player,' it caused quite a sensation, and 'Argus Junior' went round to interview Mr Margoschis on the subject, and wrote a big article thereupon, in which he referred to the schoolboy as "this experienced correspondent." How annoyed he will feel when he learns the truth!

IN MEMORIAM

● What became of the 'Memoriam cards' which related how the Villa beat Liverpool last week, and which were useless in consequence of the game being drawn? It was really painful to watch the expression on the faces of the would-be vendors as they waited for the goals that never came!

DEFENSE IS VILLA STRENGTH

● It is surprising how badly the Villa can play without in the least offending their supporters, and it is also a matter for congratulation that the defence of the team is good enough to stand the strain it was subjected to on Saturday last. The fact seems to be that a break in their training upsets the veterans, while the younger members, being able to recover quickly from the strain of a hard match, seldom give such sorry exhibitions as the older hands, and as the back division, with one exception are all young, the defence is more likely to come through the ordeal of a hard match than the attack, where one player out of form may spoil the efforts of all his companions.

MAGNIFICENT EXHIBITION

● The Villa's victory on Monday was even more brilliant than that of Saturday. Bolton Wanderers have always given a good display at Perry Barr, and have brought off more than one victory there. It seemed likely at one period of the game that the Villa were destined to be beaten, for thirty-one minutes from the finish the Boltonians were leading by two goals to nothing. But the Villa players do not lack stamina, and actually scored six points before the whistle sounded for 'Time.' It was a magnificent exhibition, and the exuberance of the spectators as the home team put on goal after goal was something to be remembered. To score six goals against such a champion custodian as Sutcliffe is a feat of which the Villans have every reason to be proud, and the Bolton goalkeeper will not forget his experiences in a hurry.

Villa backs, and presently from a kick well taken by Spencer, Devey headed across to John Cowan, who, with a very warm, oblique shot sent the ball dashing into the Liverpool net amid loud cheering, the first goal being scored at 20 minutes' play. Play was fairly even after this up to the interval, when the Villa were leading by 1 to 0.

On the re-start, Liverpool went off at a quick pace, And attacked strongly, but the Villa defence was as safe as possible, backs and half-backs all being reliable, and Whitehouse extremely cool. The Birmingham brigade soon took up the running, and from a well-placed kick by Evans, John Cowan headed over the bar. Evans pulled up the Liverpool right, and, after a fine piece of play by Athersmith, Devey skimmed the bar. A corner followed to the Villa, and six minutes from the re-start John Cowan headed the second goal for them. Liverpool played up pluckily, but were clearly held safe, Geary hitting the bar, and another shot from Cowan doing the same. Then came a brilliant piece of skill by Athersmith, who cleverly tricked Dunlop, and getting on full pace, went right through and shot a lovely goal, Storer not having a ghost of a chance. Allan made a nice attempt for Liverpool, but the ball rolled harmlessly across the front of the goal and, though they came again two or three times, once putting the ball into the net from a foul without it touching anyone – the Villa defence was always sound. The Birmingham team were playing well within themselves at the finish, and quite deserved their win by 3 goals to 0.

Aston Villa: Whitehouse; Spencer and Evans; Reynolds, James Cowan and Griffiths; Athersmith, Devey, Campbell, Wheldon and John Cowan.

Liverpool: Storer; Goldie and Dunlop; McCartney, Neill and Cleghorn; Geary, Michael, Allan, Becton and Bradshaw.

● The first League match of the season between the above clubs – postponed from the original date in consequence of the Cup ties – was played yesterday at Perry Barr before about 8,000 spectators. Several changes were made in both teams.

The Villa lost the toss, and played uphill against the wind. Smith at once made a fine run up the left and got in a nice centre, which Wheldon shot across too fast for Athersmith to reach, Bolton came down on the left, but Nicol was offside when he sent in a grand shot just wide of the mark. Athersmith, Devey, and Campbell made a pretty run, but after some tricky play the first-named put the ball out. This was followed by a smart sprint by Smith, who turned the ball over to Wheldon, the latter being very tricky, but shooting at long range just wide of the mark. Cassidy cleverly stopped Campbell, and "hands" gave the visitors a nice opening, which, however, was not utilised, Devey banging the ball out of danger, and Athersmith sprinting upfield for Smith to shoot over the bar. Bolton came down and got a foul in a useful position, followed by a corner, but Reynolds cleared in clever style, and the Villa were soon pressing again. They were repulsed, and Jack tried a long shot, which was yards over the bar. A desperate bully took place about 30 yards from the home goal, but Bolton kicked out. A smart piece of work by

Charlie Athersmith

Wheldon, Campbell, and Devey, put the ball to Athersmith, but he tried a tireless long shot in preference to a centre, which would have been more useful. Wright had a good chance, but shot wide, though immediately afterwards Spencer missed his kick and Jack, with the goal open, had no difficulty in shooting into the Villa net 16 minutes from the start. Bolton continued to have the best of it with the wind, and forced a corner, but when Reynolds missed Evans

TREASURES ON EARTH

● The Villa continue to lay up for themselves treasures on earth, in spite of the proof they have had that thieves break in and steal, for the amount of money they have earned this last month must far surpass anything in the history of the club. The Committee speak of great expenses, training, and travelling, but £2,000 takes a deal of spending in this way, and we shall look forward with confidence to the purchase of a new reserve team which shall include a few internationals during the close season.

4 APRIL 1897

JACK BACKS SUNDERLAND

● I had a chat with Jack Reynolds, the Villa half-back, the other day, when he expressed every confidence of his club winning the English Cup, in addition to the League Championship. Asked his opinion concerning the test matches, the veteran international stated that he considers Sunderland will retain their position all right, though Burnley will probably be ousted by Notts County. Should Sunderland be thrown out, he is strongly of opinion that the First Division of the League should be enlarged in order that they may retain the position, for it would be a standing disgrace to the League if a club which has accomplished such brilliant achievements as they have done during the past six years should be compelled to play with the Second Division clubs just because they have had a run of ill luck during the present season.

WHERE ARE THE PROPHETS NOW?

● Much doubt was expressed among a certain section of Aston Villa's supporters before the present season commenced as to whether the committee had acted wisely in paying such a heavy sum as £300 to the Small Heath club for the transfer of their crack left-winger, George Frederick Wheldon, and a large number of 'wiseheads' did not refrain from making public their opinion that Wheldon had seen his best days, and would be of no use to the Villa. Where are those 'prophets' now? As it has proved, the investment was one of the best the Villa have made in recent years, for the ex-Heathen has been the most consistent of as brilliant a quintette of forwards as ever stepped on a field, and is well worth every penny the League Champions paid for him. He had the honour of playing for England against Ireland at Nottingham a few weeks ago, and scored three of the goals obtained by his side. In the opinion of many competent judges he is the best inside left forward in the country, and England would have had no cause to regret it had he been chosen to play against Scotland at the Crystal Palace tomorrow. Wheldon has scored more goals for the Villa in League matches this season than any other player, the number to his credit being sixteen, Jack Devey being responsible for fifteen. In addition to being a champion footballer, Wheldon is a smart cricketer, and played for Worcestershire on several occasions last summer. He is 26 years of age, being born on November 1st, 1870, so should be of much use to the Villa club for many years to come.

FRED WHELDON

came across and cleared in grand style. Smith and Wheldon made a nice run, and the latter shot into goal, Sutcliffe fisting out. Again Sutcliffe twice threw out from Athersmith, and Wheldon under the bar shot over. Coming again, Smith shot into goal, but Sutcliffe fisted out grandly, and "hands" against Evans gave the visitors a nice opening. Wright, however, charged Wilkes before he played the ball, and was penalised, Spencer getting it away. Campbell made a beautiful run, and passed to Athersmith, who forced a corner, but Paton got the ball out, and Devey shot wide. Wheldon tried a good one, and Athersmith returned from Sutcliffe's throw-out, but the Villa were driven back, and a grand piece of passing by the visiting forwards ended in Jack shooting the second goal for Bolton. Campbell got through smartly, but only forced an unproductive corner, Sutcliffe making two magnificent saves. Reynolds then made a splendid shot, only the best of luck saving the Bolton goal. At the interval the visitors were leading by 2 goals to 0. Within a minute of the restart Smith put the ball into the Bolton goal, it rolling several inches over the line, but the referee did not allow it. Coming again Smith put the ball nicely in, but Campbell was slow and Scott cleared, whilst a moment later, from a fast attack, Reynolds hit the side of the net. Jack made a good run and shot, but Wilkes cleared, and at the other end Devey put the ball in for Sutcliffe to throw out. Still pressed, first Scott and then Somerville missed the ball, and Athersmith going right through, scored the first goal for the Villa 17 minutes from resuming. The home side were having all the best of the play now, and after Sutcliffe had twice saved in marvellous fashion, Reynolds drew level with a magnificent shot, these two points being scored within a few minutes of each other. The home team kept up the pressure continually, Sutcliffe being kept very busy, and the visiting goal having several narrow escapes. Smith worked a beautiful opening for himself, but with the goal open shot wide. Still, returning again, a fine bit of play by Smith and Wheldon put the ball to Campbell, who, with a grand shot, scored the third goal for the Villa. Within a few minutes Wheldon shot a fourth. Bolton had a turn, but were repulsed, and then the Villa were down again, a beautiful centre by Athersmith being met by Wheldon, and shot into the net for the fifth goal. Up to the finish the Villa had the best of matters, and just before the whistle blew they forced a corner on the left. The ball was beautifully placed, and Devey shot it into the net, the Villa thus winning a sensational game by 6 goals to 2.

Bolton Wanderers: Sutcliffe; Somerville and Scott; Paton, Cassidy, and Freebairn; Tannahill, Wright, Miller, Nicol and Jack.

Aston Villa: Wilkes; Spencer and Evans; Reynolds, Copwan, Griffiths; Athersmith, Devey, Campbell, Wheldon and Smith.

ENGLAND V SCOTLAND

● Tomorrow is the great day in the football world, England meeting Scotland at the Crystal Palace. As the Villa have four players in the selected teams, there will be some anxiety to see how they acquit themselves. Spencer and Athersmith are to be congratulated on getting their Scotch caps, the summit of a footballer's ambition; both of them deserve the honour, and Reynolds, though rather in the sere and yellow, has played well enough lately to justify his inclusion. The Scotch attack would have been strengthened by the inclusion of Campbell, but it is a strong side as it is, and the contest ought to be a memorable one in the annals of the game.

9 APRIL 1897

SUCCESS BY HALVES

● The one topic of conversation among all local football enthusiasts is the English Cup Final, and it is not going too far to say that there will be more natives of Birmingham in London tomorrow than there have ever been before. Aston Villa's supporters appear very confident of their favourites winning the trophy for the third time in their career, and as the 'champion footballer of the world,' Crabtree, will be able to resume his position in the team after a month's absence, and his presence should greatly increase the club's chances of victory. James Cowan and Reynolds will require a lot of passing, and it may safely be said that if the game is won by the Brums it will be the halves who are mainly responsible for it.

FORWARD STRENGTH

● The Villa forwards, four of whom are international players, have gained great notoriety for their tricky play wherever they have appeared this season, and it is difficult to see how the line could be strengthened. Johnny Campbell is undoubtedly *the* centre-forward of the year, and should by right have represented Scotland against England last week. However, the Londoners will have an opportunity of judging of his abilities tomorrow, and although he will be opposed by Holt, than whom there is no more experienced centre half-back, he is sure to give a good display. Athersmith and Devey make a splendid right wing, but the most damage will probably be done by Wheldon and John Cowan, who, though not so experienced a pair as the Everton left wing, both possess a great turn of speed, while Wheldon's shooting is terrific.

COMMITTEE BACK EVANS

● Evans does not attain his twenty-first birthday until June 13th next, and until last season he had never played at back. Both he and Welford come from Barnard Castle, Durham, and there has been a lot of discussion among Villa supporters as to which should play in the final, and though the majority would have preferred to see Welford in the team, Evans will not be dropped, the committee having every faith in him. In goal the Villa have a big advantage over their rivals. Both Whitehouse and Wilkes are superior to the Everton custodian, and at one time it was doubtful as to which one would be chosen to play in the final. Eventually it was decided to rely upon Whitehouse, and thus the Villa will have a Birmingham-born man doing duty for them between the sticks.

MAKING TRACKS FOR THE PALACE

● Tomorrow Birmingham will be deserted. Everyone who can borrow a bicycle or raise the price of a ticket will make tracks for the Crystal Palace and help the Villa to win the English Cup. Their supporters do not doubt the ability of John Devey's men to bring the pot back with them, and if all the men turn out fit and well it should prove the finest game of the year.

Saturday 27th March 1897
BOLTON WANDERERS 1, VILLA 2

● Neither side was fully representative in this return League match at Bolton, the home team being short of Somerville and Jones, and the Villa without Crabtree and Griffiths, Burton playing left half-back.

There was a strong cross wind when Bolton kicked off in the presence of 7,000 spectators. After some straggling play the Villa were the first to threaten real danger, John Cowan causing Sutcliffe to throw out, and Devey then hitting the cross-bar with a beauty. The Bolton left attacked strongly, but James Cowan came across and saved well, whilst a moment later Joyce missed a good opening from Wright. The Villa defence was hard pressed, Spencer being beaten by Jack, but the half-backs came up gallantly, and the home team were driven back, Athersmith shooting into Sutcliffe's hands and James Cowan putting the ball out. Bolton again broke away on the left, but Cassidy and Jack both missed good chances. Then from a nice run by the Villa left Campbell shot a beautiful goal, but the referee disallowed it, and attacking again, the home goal had a miraculous escape, Davis clearing with a flying kick after Sutcliffe had been beaten. Not to be denied though, Athersmith got in a lovely centre, and Wheldon rushed the ball into the net 25 minutes from the start. Jack made some good runs, but, like his comrades, was very weak in front of goal, and several capital openings were missed, whilst Wheldon, from a well placed foul by Spencer, headed the second for the Villa, the visitors leading at the interval by 2 goals to 0.

After Campbell had shot over the bar, Bolton were dangerous from a foul, Whitehouse making a brilliant save from Paton's shot. Play quietened down considerably, but from a foul erroneously given against Evans, McGeechan scored for Bolton, the shot being a good one. The Villa had the best of the remaining play, but took things very quietly, and though several good shots only just missed the posts, no more scoring took place, the Villa winning by 2 goals to 1.

Bolton: Sutcliffe; Davies and Scott; Paton, McGeechan and Freebairn; Wright, Cassidy, Joyce, Nicol and Jack.

Aston Villa: Whitehouse; Spencer and Evans; Reynolds, James Cowan and Burton; Athersmith, Devey, Campbell, Wheldon and John Cowan.

Saturday 3rd April 1897
BRISTOL & DISTRICT 0, VILLA 4

● Played on the new ground of the Eastville Rovers' Club, at Bristol, before 4,000 spectators. the Villa, who were weakly represented, kicked off, and soon pressed, but their goalkeeper was first troubled, and he saved from Brown. Wheldon beat Stone with a beauty, and the Villa subsequently took things easy. Two or three times after this the Rovers got away, and a bout of heading, followed by a corner, Gallier had his forehead cut, and had to leave the field. Almost immediately after Harvey beat Stone with a shot that he had no chance with. Half-time: – Villa, 2 goals; Bristol, 0.

The visitors kindly allowed Leese to take the place of Gallier, so that the locals turned out with a full team in the second half. This strengthened them but little, as the Villa still were able to toy with them. From a well-placed corner Burton notched a third goal for the visitors, who for some five minutes spilled down in front of the home goal, and gave Horsey and Conry, as well as Stone, plenty to do. The result was Smith very quickly put on another goal, whilst Campbell only just missed. Result: – Villa, 4 goals; Bristol, 0.

Villa: Whitehouse; Bourne and Welford; Johnstone, Burton and Crawford; Smith, Harvey, Campbell, Wheldon and John Cowan.

Aston Villa's Prospects For The Final

A CHAT WITH MR G B RAMSAY

● In the hope of obtaining some items of interest concerning the Aston Villa team and their prospects for the final tie of the English Cup competition, which takes place at the Crystal Palace this day week, a representative of the Mail yesterday had a chat with Mr. George Ramsay, whose secretarial ability has had not a little to do with the present high position the Aston Villa club occupy in first class football.

GEORGE RAMSAY

The writer knew George Ramsay when he was captain of the Villa team, in the middle of the seventies, and when he used to bound into the Perry Barr arena with a sprightliness which was the envy of his comrades and opponents. His little polo hat was always to be seen where the fight was hottest, and he it was who taught the Aston Villa eleven of the day all they know about football. George Ramsay was an enthusiast then and he is an enthusiast now.

He waxed exceedingly and judiciously, enthusiastic about the prospects of Aston Villa in the final tie. "I think we shall win the game," he said. "I made up my mind early in the season that we had a great chance of gaining both the League and the English Cup this year, and I have never had any reason for changing my mind. I based that opinion pretty much on what I saw in the second match of the season, when we went into Lancashire to play Everton. I regarded that match as one of the greatest tests we should have. I know what that journey to Everton means. I was in charge of the team that day, and saw at once what material we had at our disposal. At the close of the game I said, "This form is good enough to win us many of our matches. My prediction has come true.

"I know our form in home matches has not been true, and I should like to speak on that point. Our men are great players, and they feel that they have great reputations to keep up. This makes them unduly sensitive. When a man makes a couple of shots which are not quite up to form the crowd begin to hoot. The team feel that they are being unduly criticised throughout the match, and it makes them positively unwilling to shoot as they are able to do, as they ought to do, and as they actually do in other games. They seem frightened to try all the way as a football player ought to do. The Perry Barr crowd is undoubtedly rather too critical. When they are away they are indifferent as to what the crowd think of them, and they let fly at goal at every opportunity. This is what wins at football. A man must make some bad shots during an afternoon's football. It is undoubtedly an advantage to play at home, and the curious results we have had at Perry Barr make some explanation necessary. I have spoken to all the men about it, and they all tell the same tale, and I am fully convinced that the explanation they give is the correct one."

Proceeding to discuss the eleven individually and collectively, Mr. Ramsay said: "We have a splendidly balanced eleven this year. John Campbell, our centre, has settled down splendidly this year. He used to be a trifle slow, but now he leads the forwards capitally and he has been invaluable. John Devey, too, has played better football this year than he did last. He has rarely done badly, and with two centre men in such form the play has always been deadly. Wheldon is a man whom it is not expedient to work too much; if he trains too hard he is liable to lose his form. Our trainer is a man who is quick to note such things, and he soon found out the kind of treatment which suited him. He has been of great service. John Cowan is a clever little player, and keeps his head better than any man in our forward line. He played a rare game in the cup tie with Liverpool at

ENGLISH CUP FINAL

Saturday 10th April 1897
VILLA 3, EVERTON 2

● The final tie for the English Cup was played on Saturday at the Crystal Palace, London, the contestants being Aston Villa and Everton. Both teams were in the pink of condition when they stepped on the field in the presence of an enormous crowd of spectators, some 60,000 or 70,000 strong. The weather was fine and on winning the toss the Villa took advantage of a fair breeze and had the sun at their backs.

Everton kicked off just before four o'clock and at once pressed, but some capital heading by the Villa halves took the ball to the other end, where Holt was hurt, causing the game to be stopped a few minutes. A fine run by Milward was stopped by Spencer, and then the Everton backs were called upon to defend. The siege was raised, but Athersmith renewed the attack, and Everton were being pressed till relief came through the ball going behind. A foul against Everton ensued close in goal, but John Cowan kicked wide of the mark. Very pretty work by Devey and Campbell ended in the latter shooting wide. Milward looked like coming right through twice, but once was beautifully tackled by Spencer and a second time was offside. Fine passing between Athersmith and Devey ensued, and then a quarter of an hour from the start, Campbell, after a nice piece of dodging, scored the first goal for the Villa with a beautiful shot right at the corner of the net. Milward and Chadwick ran past the centre line, but were very cleverly pulled up by Reynolds, who headed the ball away as he fell. The Everton forwards were fast, but did not pass with the machine-like precision of the Villa, whilst they were almost invariably pulled up by the opposing halves. Hartley broke away, but he was tackled by Cowan, and following good work by Crabtree, Meechan had to kick away. A foul against the Villa afforded their rivals relief, but Athersmith was soon at work again. He only succeeded in dribbling over the goal line, however. Then Reynolds had a turn, and shot just over the bar. Hartley got an opening at the other end, but spoilt it through getting offside. Another run by Hartley caused the Villa goalkeeper to run out, Bell dashed up and scored for Everton, whilst the other two players who came into collision were winded for a time. Encouraged by their success Everton played up finely, Hartley did some very clever work, and passing to Taylor this man was fouled, and from the kick Boyle put through, the ball striking Spencer's arm. The Villa tried desperately, and from a free kick by Crabtree, John Cowan once more brought the scores level at the second attempt. Play afterwards was exceedingly fast. In trying to head away Storrier conceded a corner. This was beautifully placed by

Sheffield, he played a real cup tie game all through. Athersmith is, of course, easily the best man in the country in his position. James Cowan is still a fine tackler; and Crabtree, if able to play, as we think he will, is supremely good. Reynolds is not quite as he was, but he is an artful fellow and is more likely to play a good game in an important match than in a small one. Griffiths, if wanted, is a plucky half, and after being well coached by his companions, played a most creditable game in the second half of the match at Sheffield. Spencer is a cool, reliable back and in his own quiet style is not to be excelled, and Francis is a most serviceable defender. His play has been far too violently criticised in some quarters. He is a young, strong fellow, and if he sees the ball he feels constrained to go for it. At present his dash atones for his lack of experience. Next year he should make one of the best backs in the country. He is just the build for a good back. The criticism he has had would have taken the pluck out of most young players. There is nothing to choose between the goalkeepers, but Whitehouse is the cooler man, and will probably be played.

"Yes, I think we have a great chance. We have met Everton twice this year, and on one occasion we won and on the other we certainly should have won. Mind, I am not under-rating Everton. They had a bad time at the beginning of the season, but they are going well now, and we will meet their full strength. They will be meeting us at almost our full strength, and it will be a splendid match. Everton will not put us off our play, and we shall not put Everton off theirs. They play the same game as we do; possibly their passing is a little longer than ours. If we win we shall have accomplished a sterner feat than North End accomplished, for they were supreme; now clubs are more or less of an equality. If we beat the Blackburn Rovers on our new ground on Easter Sunday (our opening match there), we shall be sure of the League, and if a Lancashire club gives us the victory it will be significant, for we have not lost a League match in Lancashire this season."

Referring to the popularity of the Villa as a playing team, Mr. Ramsay stated that no club was in anything like such demand. They had recent applications for matches from dozens of clubs in all parts of Great Britain. "Everyone", Mr. Ramsay continued, "seems to want to see us. We have enough offers to provide three matches a day for every day after the final tie. But naturally we must restrict our programme.

"After Easter Saturday one week remains. April the 24th is the date of the Birmingham Charity Final, in which we meet the Walsall club. On the 26th we play our last League game, meeting North End at Preston. On the 28th we play the Albion at the Lower Grounds and they will share the gate. On the 29th, Thursday we go to Nottingham to meet Notts County for the benefit of Bramley. We pay all our own expenses so that Bramley will get the gross gate. It is possible that on the 30th we may play the Glasgow Rangers here for the benefit of the Indian Famine Fund, but that is not settled. Five of the men go to the International match today, Devey being the first reserve. We go to Buxton to train for the final and leave there on Friday for London, arriving at the metropolis at 6 p.m. We stop the night at Upper Norwood. We don't want people to know precisely where we are. Then we go leisurely to the Crystal Palace on Saturday morning. If fine, it will be the best and biggest final ever known, and the taking will not be far short of £3,000."

Athersmith and although Meechan threw away once Athersmith returned into the mouth of the goal and another roar went up as Wheldon gave Aston Villa the lead. Once more Hartley made another dash down the field, and passed to Milward, who had the goal at his mercy but kicked right over the bar. Everton tried hard to get on terms, but were held well in check by the Villa backs and half-backs and the interval arrived with the Villa leading by 3 goals to Everton 2.

Upon resuming Everton were the first to attack, but they could not break through the Villa defence, which was excellent, James Cowan, Crabtree and the backs especially distinguishing themselves. Taylor was particularly conspicuous, but all that ensued was a fruitless corner. At the other end Reynolds was awarded a free kick for a foul throw by Stewart, but shot the ball yards wide. Fine play by Chadwick and Taylor gave Bell a chance, but he was not ready, and Evans cleared well. A clever kick by Boyle landed

Albert Evans

the ball in front of the Aston goal, but it was sent behind the posts. Milward and Chadwick got in some nice work and in the course of a neat run Bell was fouled, Stewart took the kick, but his shot landed on the bar and bounced over. Then the Everton goal was threatened, Menham having to fist away twice from John Cowan, but eventually the ball went behind. For some little time after this play was of an even character. At one end Whitehouse saved from Bell and at the other Menham did the same from Devey. A free kick for hands against the Villa was only cleared with difficulty and then a clever run by Athersmith caused Everton to concede a corner, which Boyle got away easily. Attacking, Taylor and Bell had similar concessions at the other end, but nothing resulted, though Chadwick and Boyle each made grand shots, Whitehouse brought off brilliant saves, on the latter occasion with Crabtree in front of him. Nothing more was done and the Villa won a magnificent game by 3 goals to Everton 2.

Aston Villa: Whitehouse; Spencer and Evans; Reynolds, James Cowan and Crabtree; Athersmith, Devey, Campbell, Wheldon and John Cowan.

Everton: Menham; Meechan and Storrier; Boyle, Holt and Stewart; Taylor, Bell, Hartley, Chadwick and Milward.

● Lord Rosebury, in presenting the cup to the winners referred to the splendid game he had witnessed, which he described as a great Olympian struggle. He was certain from what he saw that to play football as he saw it played that day the highest physical attainments were necessary and an intellectual ability of no mean order. He did not know why he had been selected to present the Cup, unless it was because he was the greatest novice on the ground, but though he could not speak about the points of the game he could sincerely say that he had seen a sight that would live forever in his memory, as he was sure it would in the minds of all who had shared the enjoyment of that great struggle. The Cup was then presented to the captain of the Villa team, who made a brief reply.

THE WINNING OF THE ENGLISH CUP

● From the time the Villa committee's saloon train drew up at New Street on Saturday morning, it was evident that that genial body were very confident of the result of the great match, for the carriages were handsomely decorated with the Villa colours, (the festoons came in handy for mufflers at night), and the officials and their wives sported most gorgeous favours, which must have cost ten shillings each. Mr Campbell Orr, though he had taken the junior internationals to Glasgow the week before, had to steal another day to help to educate the Londoners. Howard Vaughton went to see how the left wing compared with the one of ten years ago: the Old Edwardians had a saloon on their own, and in fact every one who aspired to have an opinion on football boarded this train, and interviewed George Ramsay to get the last reports concerning Crabtree's fitness, and the trainer's verdict on the team's chances. It proved an expensive journey to many, but when the Palace was reached the sight of the vast crowds streaming to the football ground was worth the price, and when the teams entered the field the enclosure presented a sight never to be forgotten.

Football scribes are fond of alluding to the Crystal Palace ground as an ideal place for a match, as everyone can see in comfort, but it shouldn't be forgotten that they speak from their experience of the press box. From the stands it is all they say, but the great majority who had to stand on a grassy slope only a little less steep than the side of a house, quite innocent of barriers or any means of securing a firm footing, were far from enthusiastic concerning it, and though it was bitter cold on the stands some robust individuals who braved the slope confessed at midnight that they hadn't even then got cool, though they had finished some bottles of whisky in the attempt to do so.

Of the game little need now be said: the Villa played better than they generally do, but so did Everton, and had the latter drawn, there would have been no reason to complain. Bell in particular was a terror to the Villa defenders, and though he doesn't deserve the extravagant praise some of the London papers lavished on him, he is certainly one of the finest forwards who ever played, and lucky it was for the Villa that James Cowan was there to take him in charge when he grew troublesome. On the Villa side there were no failures, though Crabtree had hardly recovered from his recent injury. I thought he played with more fire in the last twenty minutes, but, speaking to him after the match, he said that it was only then he felt his leg, it ached badly, perhaps it was the pain that spurred him on.

Athersmith's speed delighted the crowd: they called him 'Charley's Aunt, still running,' and Devey and Campbell played better than they have done this season, the latter especially having hard lines with some grand attempts. Reynolds is the most popular man in the team with a London crowd, who cannot understand why the Villa have preferred Chatt to him. The fact is that, though he doesn't do as much work as Cowan, he looks to be doing twice as much, and his wonderful trickery was greatly in evidence on Saturday, for he kept Milward and Chadwick pretty harmless.

Speaking to Crabtree after the match, he expressed the opinion that Everton deserved two goals far more in the second half than they did in the first, while his admiration for James Cowan was boundless. I have met people who, after a careful study of the descriptions of the game, were of opinion that the Villa always had the match in hand, but the truth is that their supporters never had a more anxious time than in the last half-hour, and the referee's whistle was the sweetest music they have heard for a long time.

Euston at midnight was a scene of uproarious gaiety. Men who had been two hours and a half reaching Victoria from the Palace forgot their grievances in congratulating the committee and each other, Mrs Archie Hunter was beaming, but Mr James Lees was as solemn as an owl; afraid to smile

LEAGUE DIVISION ONE

Saturday 17th April 1897
VILLA 3, BLACKBURN ROVERS 0

● Aston Villa opened their new football enclosure at the Aston Lower Grounds on Saturday with the return League match against Blackburn Rovers. Unfortunately the weather was terribly wet, rain falling in torrents. Still there was a large crowd, quite 14,000 spectators being present, including a large contingent of excursionists from Blackburn.

The Villa played their Cup team, and had a splendid reception on entering the new enclosure, which was spoken of in the highest terms by everyone present. The Rovers were at full strength, with the exception of Dewar, and the game was a capital one to watch, the home side showing much better form than some people expected. The football was quite first-class, and though the visitors were overmatched, they played in the pluckiest style, Proudfoot and Campbell amongst the forwards, and the whole of the half-backs doing particularly well. The first danger came from the Villa right, where Athersmith and Devey were

James Cowan

in their happiest mood. The former forced a corner from Killean, but it was cleared for a time. Campbell (Villa), however, obtained possession in mid-field, and making a splendid individual dribble through the whole of his opponents finished a superb piece of play by shooting a goal. No finer effort has been seen for a long time, and Campbell was enthusiastically cheered for his fine play. Not long afterwards Campbell tried another good shot, but he just missed, whilst James Cowan shot over the bar. Proudfoot on the other hand made a couple of fine runs, but though playing a grand game, he was knocked off the ball before he could shoot. Nicol then got through and shot into the net, but he was clearly offside, and the point was not allowed. Athersmith forced a couple of unproductive corners, and then John Cowan sent in a beauty, which Killean tried to stop, but it went off him into the net. A beautifully combined run by the Villa forwards deserved a better fate than for Devey to put the ball just over the bar, and though the Rovers tried hard, the interval arrived with the Villa leading by 2 goals to 0.

On restarting the Villa at once pressed, and Devey sent in a grand shot, which would have certainly beaten Ogilvie, but Brandon happened to be handy and got the ball away cleverly. Ogilvie, who kept goal well, stopped a warm shot from Athersmith following on a corner, after which the visitors attacked in spirited fashion, but could not beat the home defence, which was excellent, Spencer quite excelling himself. Wheldon missed a good opening from Athersmith, but directly afterwards a pretty piece of combination left the Villa in front of the visitors' goal, where Campbell and Devey were conspicuous, the upshot being that Killean, in endeavouring to clear, again put the ball into his own goal. Play continued to be fast and attractive, notwithstanding the heavy ground, Proudfoot, Anderson, Booth and Brandon playing finely for the visitors. Hargreaves tried a good shot, which was well cleared, and at the other end Ogilvie several times got the ball away from dangerous attempts, Athersmith and Devey being particularly busy. Try as the would, the Rovers could not penetrate the home defence, whilst John Cowan added a fourth goal, but was given off-side. Towards the close Blackburn made renewed efforts, and must have scored but for the fine play of Spencer, Evans, and Whitehouse. Nothing more was done, however, and the Villa won their first match on their new ground in clever style by 3 goals to 0.

Blackburn Rovers: Ogilvie; Brandon and Killean; Booth, Crompton and Anderson; Nicol, Hargreaves, Proudfoot, Wilkie and Campbell.

Aston Villa: Whitehouse; Spencer and Evans; Reynolds, James Cowan and Crabtree; Athersmith, Devey, Campbell, Wheldon and John Cowan.

lest he should never stop. Crabtree and Reynolds were also there, the latter as fresh as paint and looking as though he had just come out for an airing. One misguided enthusiast suggested inviting him into the carriage to play nap, but was restrained by cooler heads, "for if he comes in here," said one, "he'll go home with our shirts," so that football is not the only game he can play. New Street too, was alive when the train steamed in at half-past three, quite an army of men being there with football editions oblivious of the fact that London, too, has evening papers, with men on there (from Birmingham) quite able to cope with the craze for descriptive reports on the great match, and if records were established here, I should imagine that the *Star* and *Evening News* made records in London, too, for they were selling like wildfire.

16 APRIL 1897

SMALL HEATH UNSEEDED

● The supporters of the Small Heath Football Club are greatly annoyed that their pets should have been left out of the 'exempted eighteen' for next season's English Cup competition, especially when Walsall are included. When it is remembered that the Heathens rarely get further than the first round, however, it will be recognised that the Association have acted quite fairly in compelling them to take part in the qualifying round.

WHAT WE HEAR...

↝ *That the English League v Scottish League match next season will be played at the Aston Lower Grounds.*

↝ *That the Sports Argus had a big sale at Euston Station on Saturday midnight.*

↝ *That the Old Villans' carnival at Perry Barr tomorrow (Good Friday) should be well patronised.*

↝ *That the last football match has been played at Perry Barr.*

↝ *That four Aston Villa players, viz., Athersmith, Devey, Crabtree, and Spencer, have been chosen to represent the English League against the Scottish League at Glasgow on Saturday week.*

THE MC AT THE FINAL

A CHAT WITH MR LEWIS

● Ere the result of the historical final – fitly closed with the presentation of the trophy to that sterling player, John Devey, by our ex-Premier and the brilliant Foreign Secretary of the last Government – is finally signed, sealed, and delivered to the pigeon-hole of the Football Association and the files of the newspapers, a word from Mr John Lewis must be entered, or it would be an incomplete document indeed. Said he of the battle, when it was over and done: The first half was splendidly fought, but the second half was not nearly so fair, the

JOHN LEWIS

defence on both sides proving too good for the attack. To sum up, the Villa deserved to win, being slightly the better team. The backs kicked and tackled splendidly, and the halves followed well up, Reynolds being the pick. The forwards all played hard and well, and although perhaps Athersmith was most prominent, still I cannot single him out for special praise. With regard to the Everton team, I do not think that Menham can justly be blamed, for he had not the ghost of a chance with any of the goals scored. The backs played well, Storrier being the best; indeed, he was throughout

Monday 19th April 1897
VILLA 5, WOLVES 0

● The return match between these clubs was played yesterday at Aston Lower Grounds, at the conclusion of the cycling sports, their being quite 35,000 spectators present. The visitors won the toss, and played with a stiffish breeze at their backs.

The Villa, however, at once ran down, and from Athersmith's centre Devey put the ball across goal, John Cowan, on the post, putting it outside. The Wolves went up on the right, playing cleverly, but the ball was put outside, and the Villa returned to the attack, a foul giving a nice opening for Reynolds to shoot over the bar. Coming again, however, a beautiful run by the home forwards ended in Athersmith centring, and Campbell turning the ball over to John Cowan, who shot a fine goal five minutes from the start. On restarting, the Wolves pressed severely, forcing two corners, but they were well cleared, and a brilliant piece of play Campbell deserved a better fate than to shoot just over the bar. The game continued very fast, the Wolves playing up in the most gallant fashion. The ball travelling rapidly from end to end, Wood making a fine run, but only to be pulled up by a grand piece of play on the part of Evans. a beautiful run by Wheldon and John Cowan was applauded, but Eccles cleared, and more interesting play followed in midfield, the Wolves getting the better of it and forcing Whitehouse to throw out twice in quick succession. The Villa again got away on the right, Athersmith and Devey forcing a corner, which was unproductive. The Wolves had another run, chiefly through the fine play of Owen, who finished up with a lovely shot, which was splendidly saved by Whitehouse. Spencer and Reynolds cleared another attack by the Wolves, who were showing great dash, but when they came again they only succeeded in driving the ball out. Then the Villa came down in a body, and Athersmith brought Tennant to his knees with a fine shot. A beautiful run and centre by Wheldon was got away by Fleming and when James Cowan was left in possession he shot a long way wide of the mark. A little later the Villa were pressing again, but some pretty play by the forwards was neutralised by a weak shot on the part of Burton. Another grand run by Devey and Athersmith only resulted in the ball being driven over, and a foul in midfield was not utilised. The Wolves attacked again in vigorous fashion, but though they did some pretty work, the Villa defence was sound. Give and take play followed, for although the Villa were much the cleverer in combination, they were met by rare resolution and dash, and try as they would they could not get through. John Cowan forced a corner, and another fell to Athersmith, but neither was improved upon, and the Wolves rushing up the right, attacked strongly, only, however, to be turned back by the grand defence of the home side. One piece of play by Reynolds – when he turned a somersault, but still retained possession of the ball, was loudly cheered. A lively centre by Athersmith just skimmed the front of the bar, and John Cowan could not meet it to head it in, the interval arriving with the Villa leading by 1 goal to 0.

On resuming, the Villa, with the wind at their backs, were speedily on the aggressive. Athersmith forced a corner, which James Cowan put the ball back to Devey, who shot the second goal a couple of minutes from the restart. The Wanderers had a turn, but nothing came of it, and the Villa right going up again, Reynolds put the ball across, but Wheldon drove it out. Within a few minutes the Villa were attacking again, and John Cowan, cleverly gaining possession, he beat the opposing backs, and finished a fine individual effort by shooting a pretty goal right into the corner of the net. The Wolves then had a turn, but though they got close in, Owen's shot was a yard wide of the mark. A brilliant piece of play by Spencer, when he dispossessed Smith, was loudly cheered. Very interesting exchanges followed, and after the Villa had twice the surprise of the match. Meechan spoiled his otherwise good play by jumping, which had to be penalised. Stewart played well throughout, and though Holt was not up to the work in the early stages, the little man improved as the game progressed. Boyle, however, never seemed in a happy mood. The only forwards who did themselves justice were Hartley and Milward, none of the others playing up to their real form.

J. L. is never too busy to spare half an hour in chatting about football. Allude to the ancient aspect of the game, and he is ready. Mention the modern, and he is willing. He has a close acquaintance with both, and will tell you more about their strengths and failings in five minutes than can most men. If you lead him on he will spend an hour in discussing the principles and ramifications of his pet pastime.

As you all know, Mr Lewis was, in a non-combatant sense, the central figure on the Crystal Palace playground on Saturday afternoon, directing the ceremonies of Aston Villa v Everton for the English Cup. A few days after his appointment as referee for the Final was notified I sought him out, and invited him to be formally interviewed.

I WAS MOBBED!

"What do you want to know?" he enquired. I strapped him securely in the confessional chair, and said he couldn't be released until he had given me the material for an article one column in length, and entitled *'Reminiscences of a Referee'*. Then I told him to collect his thoughts and relate some of his most amusing experiences – 'mobbing,' for instance, and pleasant little incidents of that sort.

"Yes, I've been mobbed," said J. L.; "and like many another referee who has experienced that distinction, I didn't deserve it. The first time was at Bury. Accrington were the visitors, and were winning easily. Bury never scored, nor did they dispute any of Accrington's goals; but the spectators kept shouting to the Accrington umpire (it was in the old umpire days) to come off the playground outside the touch-line. He wouldn't go, and then they shouted to me to make him: but I had no power to send him off, so he stayed where he was."

"Well?"

"Well, the crowd waited until the game was over. The umpire got away somewhere, but they took it out of me. Not very badly. There was a bit of rough hustling, but I managed to get off without a broken head. On another occasion Accrington were playing Darwen at Darwen. I forget what match it was, but I remember the bother arose over a goal I disallowed Darwen for off-side. Horne was keeping goal, and Hugh Richmond was standing off-side a yard or so away from him, when up came Marshall with the ball and let fly at goal. The shot scored, but Richmond obstructed the goalkeeper, and so I disallowed it. Well, 'after the ball' the crowd corrected my ruling. You had to pass right through the spectators in those days to get to the dressing-rooms. They made a lane for the players and officials, and as I went through they hacked and punched me right and left a good one. No; I've never been ducked that I remember. If I had, I should probably recollect it, so you can put down 'No' to that question."

TIP FOR THE TOP

Harking back a bit, Mr Lewis said it was sixteen or seventeen years since he first wielded the whistle. He began in small matches, and gradually got into the better ones and since then he had controlled the proceedings at some scores of matches – League games, Cup ties, 'friendlies' and encounters which were anything but friendly, and which needed prompt and punitive measures to keep the players under control. "I have been invited to referee in International matches, but it so happened that I was also engaged in semi-finals on those occasions, and I preferred to officiate in the Cup ties. It is two years since I refereed in the Cup final at the Palace between Aston Villa and West Bromwich Albion. That was a pleasant game right through, and I hadn't the least bother."

And that reminded me that several months ago, when the clubs of the League had revealed a fair proof of their 'form,' I asked Mr Lewis what was

attacked in dangerous fashion, the Wolves got through and forced a corner. Reynolds got the ball away in good style, and John Cowan made off nicely, but Eccles pulled him up, and the Villa could do nothing better than shoot outside. The Wolves, nothing daunted, played up in gallant fashion, and Reynolds, when hard pressed, was lucky to find the ball kicked out. Reynolds a moment later put the ball to Athersmith, who raced away in grand style, but Eccles came across and cleared splendidly. Not to be denied, however, the Villa right came again in most brilliant fashion, and after some lovely passing, and despite the fine defence of Fleming and Tennant, Campbell scored the fourth goal – a perfect gem. The Wolves got down by pretty play, and from a fine centre by Wood, Beale shot just outside the posts. After another nice run by the whole of the home front rank Wheldon brought Tennant to his knees with a grand shot. Still playing in the pluckiest style, the Wolves forced a couple of corners, but they were not improved upon, and Campbell running up field got a foul in a good position. The ball was

Howard Spencer

well placed, but Tennant threw out, and the Wanderers immediately ran down the left, Wood forcing a corner. This was got away, and the Villa forwards, getting into swing again, Campbell finished a beautiful run by shooting hard into the net. Twice after this Tennant had to save, which he did in workmanlike fashion, and nothing more being scored, the Villa won by 5 goals to 0.

Wolverhampton Wanderers: Tennant; Eccles and Fleming; Griffiths, Owen and Malpass; Tonks, McMain, Beale, Wood and Smith.

Aston Villa: Whitehouse; Spencer and Evans; Reynolds, James Cowan and Burton; Athersmith, Devey, Campbell, Wheldon and John Cowan.

MAYOR'S CHARITY CUP

Saturday 24th April 1897
ASTON VILLA 1, WALSALL 1

● These clubs met on Saturday at the Lower Grounds in the competition for the Mayor of Birmingham's Charity Cup, the weather being fine, and the attendance about 8,000 strong. The Villa were short of Spencer, Crabtree, Athersmith, and Devey. Prior to the match a contingent of members of the Birmingham Athletic Institute gave a most interesting gymnastic and athletic display under the direction of Professor Chase.

Walsall won the toss, and, playing with the wind, at once ran up to the Villa goal, but James Cowan relieved, and Campbell passing to John Cowan, the latter forced a corner. This was unproductive, but the Villa still pressed until C. L. Aston cleared. A couple of free-kicks for hands put Walsall on the aggressive again, but they only succeeded in heading the ball out on the left, though Whitehouse had to twice throw away. Smith got off nicely on the right, and after some pretty play Harvey hit the bar with a grand shot. The ball dropped in front of the posts, and Bunyan cleared cleverly before Campbell could get on it, the latter stumbling. John Cowan was off-side when he looked like getting away, but going up in a body the Villa attacked strongly, several shots being rained in, but splendidly cleared by the visiting backs and goalkeeper. A corner followed, which Bunyan fisted away from under the bar, and some interesting play followed in midfield, Walsall by their dash making up for the superior skill of the others. A foul against the Villa was easily cleared, and a tricky piece of play by Smith, which forced a corner, was applauded. Another followed to John Cowan, and after a grand piece of play by Smith, who got in a nice centre, Wheldon shot a lovely goal 14 minutes from the start. The Villa continued to have the best of matters, both Smith and James

his 'tip' for the League championship. "Aston Villa," he replied, without hesitation; and then he added, "And if they got the League championship they'll win the Cup – now mark my words."

"And how does it feel to referee in a final with a little crowd of fifty or sixty thousand people looking on."

"No different to any other match, that I know of. You don't need to bother with the fifty or sixty thousand. Just keep your eyes on the ball and the twenty-two players, and you're right enough. With a knowledge of the game and its rules, and the little tricks sometimes adopted by players to cover their transgressions, you cannot go far wrong."

Mr Lewis has the reputation of being known as a 'strong' referee – prompt to penalise where he considers it necessary, and one of the sort to stand no nonsense from players. I questioned him on this point, and he said he was seldom bothered by refractory players. Now and again, when his ruling does not suit a peppery Scot or Englishman, he receives a 'back answer' of a sarcastic character; but a discreet silence turns away wrath in such cases.

On referees and refereeing in general J. L. expresses himself with engaging frankness. "There are lots of referees who have a perfect theoretical knowledge of the rules and how they should be administered, yet who are rank failures at enforcing them when they step on the field. Examinations would not, I believe, be of any use in regard to referees. It is simply a constitutional inability to grasp a situation which suddenly occurs in the progress of play and decide promptly there and then whether it is right or wrong."

"Suppose there were examinations and candidates who passed the test proved unequal to their duties when they got on the field, what remedy do you suggest?"

"There is no remedy."

"But do you believe in linesmen sharing the responsibility of referees?"

"Certainly not. I think neutral linesmen are being made a use of by certain referees, that was never intended when they were appointed. It is not the duty of referees to consult them upon every goal that is scored, and neither is it the duty of a referee, when he is satisfied in his own mind upon a certain point – say a foul calling for a penalty kick – to call one or both linesmen into consultation before giving a decision."

"Just my sentiments, Mr Lewis. What about the rules? Are they definite enough for the purpose of referees?"

"I think they are. Referees should administer the spirit while observing the strict letter of the rules."

Like many other old footballers whose experiences must be chock-full of interesting reminiscences, Mr Lewis could only recall one or two off-hand. "An amusing goal was once scored at Accrington against the Rovers. A free kick was given, and the ball hit the bar and dropped underneath, and a goal was allowed."

"How's that?"

"That's just what Walter Duckworth, the Rovers' umpire, wanted to know from the referee. 'How can it be a goal' he said, 'without the ball hitting another player?' The referee told him the crossbar was a player. 'Is he,' said Walter, 'Then what the d–––– is he doing up there?' Sam Ormerod, the present Manchester City secretary, was the umpire for Accrington, and he it was who claimed the goal, and the referee who awarded it was Mr Haslam, of Bolton."

"Just one more question, and then I'll let you off. What are the Football Association to do to get good referees?"

"Suspend all those who do not see the game played according to the laws," said the referee of the Final, as he rose from the confessional chair; "and in that case there will be a rare lot of 'em out of work."

John Lewis has all the characteristics of a good referee. Quick to see, prompt to act, decisive in his rulings, he is one of the strongest referees on the roll. Being mortal, he sometimes makes mistakes, but he has the merit of being able to stick to them, and this virtue he commends to all who aspire to become 'strong men' in the ranks of the referees.

Cowan narrowly missing scoring. Walsall got another foul against Reynolds, but put the ball into the net without its having touched anyone, whilst a moment later a nice run by Horrobin ended in Johnson shooting over the bar. Attacking again, the visitors made matters very warm for the Villa, whose goal had a lucky escape from a vigorous onslaught. A brilliant run by the Villa forwards ended in John Cowan shooting right across the goal, the ball passing just outside the posts, which a moment later the same player sent in a real beauty, which Bunyan saved at the expense of an unproductive corner. The Walsall goalkeeper twice threw out directly afterwards, and John Cowan skimmed the bar from some nice play by Wheldon. From a foul Walsall made a splendid attempt to score, but Whitehouse defended in his best style, and twice go the ball away with a crowd of opponents on him. Nothing more was done up to the interval, when the Villa led by a goal to nothing.

John Cowan

On resuming, nice play by Cowan and Wheldon ended in Smith hitting the side of the net, whilst at the other goal Whitehouse kicked out from under the bar. From another foul Walsall again put the ball into the net without its having touched anyone, and they also forced a corner, from which the Villa had a narrow escape. Coming again, however, they attacked strongly, the forwards playing a vigorous game, and as the result of some nice play Copeland headed into the net, making the scores level. Smith at once got clean away, and shot into goal, but Bunyan made a miraculous save, and the ball a second time rolled right across the front of the Walsall goal, but passed outside. Then Wheldon twice hit the bar in quick succession, the visiting goal having the luckiest of escapes. Interesting exchanges followed, and the Villa getting up again, Cowan headed over from a centre by Smith, whilst Bunyan brought off a couple of fine saves. The Villa pressed continuously, but could not score, and the game ended in a draw of 1 goal each. It will be re-played next Friday evening, the last day of the football season.

Walsall: Bunyan; Pears and C. L. Aston; Holmes, Wilkes and Taggart; Horrobin, J. Aston, Griffin, Copeland and Johnson.

Aston Villa: Whitehouse; Bourne and Evans; Reynolds, James Cowan and Burton; Smith, Harvey, Campbell, Wheldon and John Cowan.

LEAGUE DIVISION ONE
Monday 26th April 1897
PRESTON NORTH END 0, VILLA 1

● The last game of the season upon the Deepdale ground was played between these teams last night before about 3,000 spectators. The Villa had a full team, but Preston were without Smith, Pratt, Orr, and Stevenson, there being three reserve men in the forward rank. The weather was lovely, and the ground hard and dry.

North End won the toss and had a fairly strong breeze in their favour, but the Villa were the first to become dangerous, Sanders only stopping Wheldon as he was about to shoot. The same wing tried again, and John Cowan gave Trainer a handful which he disposed of very coolly. The next shot Trainer had to stop came from Evans at long range, but then the Preston left made a dash, and Evans had to rush over to help Spencer out of a difficulty. Midfield work followed, neither side exerting itself unduly, and although the Villa were manifestly the better lot, Trainer had no dangerous shots to deal with. Then North End got a free kick close in, and the ball seemed safe to go into the net off Sanders's head, but Whitehouse pulled down the bar, and it glided over the other end. Devey was penalised for charging Trainer, and an animated dialogue between that player and the referee caused a good deal of excitement among the crowd. Two more attacks by

DOUBLE EVENT

● The eight thousand Birmingham excursionists who went to London to see Aston Villa win the English Cup on Saturday had no cause to regret making the journey. The game was one of the finest expositions of football seen this season, and a better final tie could not have been wished for. The Villans have brought off the 'double event,' winning both the League Championship and the English Cup in one season, a feat which has only been accomplished previously by Preston North End, and their cup of joy is full to the brim. The club's performances during the past four seasons are without parallel, and are worthy of a special par. all to themselves.

1893-94 – League Championship
1894-95 – English Cup
1895-96 – League Championship
1896-97 – English Cup and League Championship

FIRST APPEARANCE

● The Villa open their new ground on Saturday, when Blackburn Rovers pay them a visit, and if there are not at least twenty thousand spectators to give a right royal reception to the champions on their first appearances at the 'Lower' it will indeed be a big surprise.

MAN OF THE MATCH

● The best player on the field at the Crystal Palace was, without a doubt, Jack Reynolds. The veteran only gained his place in the first team on account of the injury to Bob Chatt a few weeks ago, yet he has shown such brilliant form since that he was selected to represent England against both Wales and Scotland, and came out of both games with credit to himself and his club. Reynolds has played in four English Cup finals, and has been on the winning side on each occasion, a performance which no other player can boast of.

THE TRAIN WAITING...

The London, Brighton and South Coast Railway may be a good line to travel upon on ordinary occasions, but I trust that it will be long ere I have occasion to avail myself of its advantages again. After the match was over I journeyed from the Crystal Palace to Victoria, a distance of about nine miles, and we actually took two hours and ten minutes to go that far. Before the train started the occupants of the carriage in which I travelled sang "Now we shan't be long!" but we were – such a very, very long time!

NEVER AGAIN

● I shall never feel inclined to grumble at the Perry Barr trams again. They are not in the same street for slowness with the L. B. and S. C. trains.

TICKETS, PLEASE!

● The journey home was rather uneventful. Everyone – or nearly everyone – was fatigued with the day's exertions, and most of the travellers slept 'the sleep of the just' until the call for 'Tickets, please!' aroused them from their slumbers.

QUESTIONS...

☞ *Why did not the Mail send papers to Euston?*

☞ *Didn't the Argus score over this?*

☞ *And who counted the gate for the sporting papers?*

☞ *What is the difference between twenty-eight thousand and fifty thousand?*

the Villa van neutralised by off-side, and a fine run by Devey was spoiled by a capital tackle by Dunn. North End pressed in a desultory manner, but Spencer and Evans had no difficulty in keeping them off. Crabtree and Brown jumped into the air together to get the ball, and the latter getting the worst of the encounter, Mr Bye awarded a free kick to North End, which led to some exciting passages before Reynolds cleared his lines with a huge kick. A very pretty run by the Villa forwards followed, Campbell finally having an open goal and plenty of time to steady himself for his shot. The ball, however, was met at the top corner by Trainer in fine style. Some very fine defensive work by Evans followed, but North End continued this attack for several minutes, Sanders putting the ball into the net from a free kick without touching another man. Athersmith gave the spectators a touch of his quality in a long sprint with Dunn, whom he beat easily, but Tait got in the way of Campbell's shot although Devey followed with a swift one along the ground, which brought Trainer to his knees. Once more Campbell was placed in possession with a clear goal and nobody to hamper him, but he shot a foot too high, and, rushing away, the Preston forwards dashed into goal, and only just missed scoring. Brown was penalised for charging Whitehouse when the ball was out of play, and from the free-kick the Villa got up, and Athersmith centring, Wheldon hooked the ball into the net at close-range, Trainer only just touching the ball. Half-time: Villa, 1 goal; Preston, 0.

The second half opened tamely, the spectators after a time becoming impatient, and calling upon the teams to play up. From a free-kick Campbell got the ball in a scrimmage under the bar, but was so slow in shooting that Holmes took the ball from him. Then Holmes was penalised for a foul throw, and Devey put in a good ground shot, which compelled Trainer to run half way to the corner before he could clear. Rushing back, North End fairly swarmed round Whitehouse, who repelled shots in rapid succession from Sanders, Henderson, and Pearce. A spell of play followed in front of Trainer, but the Villa forwards showed no great dash, and, although Athersmith and Cowan each dropped in centres, they were not improved upon. For a long time there was nothing of interest to chronicle, the Villa being content with their lead, and North End unable to make any headway through the weakness of their forwards. James Cowan once nearly beat Trainer with a swift, low shot which the goalkeeper muffed, but the Villa forwards were too far back to take advantage of it. Then Preston attacked, and Whitehouse had twice to fist away headed shots from Henderson, and kick away another from Blyth. At the other end Dunn jumped right upon Devey's back, and a vigorous claim was made for a penalty-kick, which the referee disregarded. Then the whistle blew with the score: – Villa, 1 goal; North End, 0.

Villa: Whitehouse; Spencer and Evans; Reynolds, James Cowan and Crabtree; Athersmith, Devey, Campbell, Wheldon and John Cowan.

North End: Traine; Tait and Dunn; Blyth, Sanders and Holmes; Eccleston, Pearce, Brown, Boyd and Henderson.

MAGNIFICENT NEW GROUND

● As far as the convenience of the spectators is concerned, the Villa's new ground is a magnificent one, and if it is ever finished, there will be no ground to equal it, save only the great enclosure at the Crystal Palace. But many of the members have an uneasy suspicion that the excellence of the playing portion has been somewhat sacrificed for the sake of the cycling track, and they are anything but pleased that the committee should have gone to the expense of providing one and then to let it on such terms as give the fortunate lessees a chance of booming a new company with the lease as a capital asset. Moreover, though everything possible in the way of drainage has been introduced, the downward slope all round will, in wet weather, tend to turn the field into a lake, as was seen last Saturday, when, though the rainfall was certainly not heavy, pools of water were rather numerous there. The ground is rather narrower than the Perry Barr one, which will make it more difficult for the wing men to get away, though this didn't seem to make much difference in the match against the Rovers, for rarely have the team played so well, Athersmith, Campbell, and Devey among the forwards, and James Cowan and Spencer behind, playing at their very best. The combination of Devey and Athersmith is something to wonder at, no wing now playing comes near them, and though Devey is something of a veteran, we shall despair of ever finding another player capable of feeding his speedy partner as judiciously as he does.

NOT FOOLS

● It is gratifying to learn that most of the Aston Villa players have been signed up for next season, despite all rumours to the effect that several of them had decided to change their quarters. The players are not such fools as certain football agents took them for: they know when they are well off, and are wise enough to appreciate the benefits which they enjoy through being connected with the premier Birmingham club.

WHERE WAS WELFORD?

● The general opinion of Villa supporters concerning the exclusion of Welford from the team against Walsall last week would probably surprise the committee. Whatever the offences of the player may have been, his punishment has been duly meted out, and the action of the officials in leaving him out of the team in favour of Bourne was very severely criticised by the crowd. It is quite likely that there will be a 'rumpus' on the subject at the annual general meeting, for Welford has numerous admirers, and it is quite time the public were informed of the real season he has been excluded.

WHAT WE HEAR...

☞ *That Aston Villa's form in the holiday matches has been really astounding.*

☞ *That to score eight goals to nothing against two such clubs as Blackburn Rovers and Wolverhampton Wanderers is a feat of which they may well be proud.*

☞ *That Aston Villa play their last League match on Monday, when they visit Preston.*

MORE QUESTIONS...

☞ *Will Jimmy Welford be with Aston Villa next season?*

☞ *Are the local pressmen to be provided with proper accommodation at Aston Lower Grounds?*

☞ *How many new players have Aston Villa booked for next season?*

VILLA PLAYERS BENEFIT MATCH

Wednesday 28th April 1897

VILLA 3, ALBION 1

● A match was played between these teams at Aston Lower Grounds last evening for the benefit, the advertisements stated, of the players of the home club in honour of their having won the English Cup and the League Championship. The attendance at the most would not number more than a thousand, so that after the Albion have had their share of the takings the Cup winners will not derive any very considerable amount of benefit.

The Villa, taking matters easy, soon showed to advantage, and after about ten minutes' play Devey completely beat Reader. For some time the Villa found no reason to play seriously – a fact of which they took the fullest advantage, to the great amusement of the crowd. Richards at last got away, and seemed likely to score, but Spencer collared him, and sent the ball to the other end, where a nice bit of play between Wheldon and Cowan enabled the latter to centre, Devey headed the pass through. McLeod gave Whitehouse a hot one, which he had to take very seriously, his save being clever. The Villa custodian was again called upon by both Watson and McLeod, and the latter, coming again, scored. Half-time: – Villa, 2; Albion, 1.

Athersmith was the first to look like scoring on the resumption, but after a good run he only managed to put into Reader's hands. Wheldon next got away on the left, and from his centre Devey for the third time scored. Down at the other end Watson got in a shot which Whitehouse very cleverly saved, and for a short time the Albion were dodging about in front of goal, but they failed to score. When the ball was taken to the opposite end Wheldon put it past Reader, but was declared off-side. Flewitt gave Whitehouse a nasty shot to deal with, but Whitehouse was systematically clever. The game ended: – Villa, 3 goals; Albion, 1.

Aston Villa: Whitehouse; Spencer and Evans; Reynolds, Cowan and Crabtree; Athersmith, Devey, Campbell, Wheldon and Cowan.

West Bromwich Albion: Reader; Horton and Cave; Perry, McManus and Banks; Watson, Flewitt, McLeod, Richards and Garfield.

BRAMLEY BENEFIT MATCH

Thursday 29th April 1897

NOTTS COUNTY 1, VILLA 2

● This friendly match was played at Nottingham for the benefit of Bramley, the Notts half-back, who had his leg broken in the English Cup-tie against the Villa at Birmingham in February. There were 3,000 spectators, and Bramley will benefit substantially. The game was fairly interesting throughout, though neither side was at full strength. Notts had slightly the best of the game, but the Villa just won by 2 goals to 1.

MAYOR'S CHARITY CUP REPLAY

Friday 30th April 1897

VILLA 1, WALSALL 2

● The Walsall and Aston Villa clubs met yesterday at the Lower Grounds in the replayed final tie for the Mayor of Birmingham's Charity Cup, the former match having ended in a draw of one goal each. Although this was the last match of the season and both clubs were fully represented, there were not more than a thousand spectators.

The game was not a very interesting one, the Villa

☞ *Do the committee mean having a capable reserve team?*

☞ *What are Jack Devey's chances of playing for Warwickshire now that he has been reinstated an amateur?*

☞ *How much had the cement track at the 'Lower' to do with poor Harris's untimely death?*

☞ *Could the accident have occurred on a cinder track?*

☞ *When will Aston Villa let their supporters see the new English Cup?*

☞ *Have not Sykes and Co. discovered its whereabouts yet?*

☞ *Has the Aston Villa club house been as well patronised by the players during the past season as it might have been?*

30 APRIL 1897

HERE COMES KING CRICKET

● The football season dies tonight, and King Cricket will once again rule the world of sport for a brief four months. The end of the winter pastime has not come a day too soon, for everyone – spectators, committee-men, and the players themselves – are thankful that the time when they can 'rest' is so close at hand. The Aston Villa players have had a busy time of it lately. On Saturday they opposed Walsall, on Monday they played their last League match of the season at Preston, a friendly game with West Bromwich Albion took place at the 'Lower' on Wednesday, yesterday they played Notts County at Trent Bridge for Bramley's benefit, while this (Friday) evening they meet Walsall again to settle who is to have possession of the Mayor of Birmingham's Charity Cup. Thus endeth the present season!

BETTER MEN WON

● As the Villa had four men, and the Albion one, in the team which lost at Glasgow on Saturday, the defeat becomes a personal matter with us, and our critics have been busy ever since explaining how they came to lose. Perhaps it would be simpler to admit that they met better men, but it would be vain to expect Midlanders to believe that there are men who can stop Athersmith and Bloomer, and others who can get by Crabtree and Spencer.

HARD ON SMITH

● While the fliers were disporting themselves in Glasgow, the remnant were being hard put to it to raise a gallop against Walsall, for the work of the season has at length told on the majority of them, and it is just as well that it finishes to-day and they can take a well-earned rest. The poor character of the Villa Reserves was strikingly manifested in this match, two of those tried seeming as much out of place as schoolboys would be among their big brothers. Smith and Burton were, of course better, but they have been trained in the first team, and it is a pity they haven't better companions, if they are to be condemned to the second. Smith was the best forward on the field on Saturday, and to my mind there are few left wingers to equal him even now, and it is hard lines on him to have no regular place in the League eleven.

COMMEMORATIVE MEDALS

● At the annual meeting of the Aston Villa Shareholders some time back, it was decided to give the directors and other chief officers of the club gold medals to celebrate the club's winning of the English Cup and League Championship last season. A special design was drawn by Messrs P. Vaughton and Sons, of Great Hampton Row, Birmingham, and the medals were made by them. The medals are of high standard gold, and of much more than the ordinary value. On the obverse side, the recognition of services rendered is expressed, and on the reverse side are representations of the two chief trophies of the Association Football world.

players, after their hard week's work, not exerting themselves, and in the end they suffered defeat by 2 goals to 1. The Villa lost the toss, and kicked off against the wind. Walsall was the first to press, and after Whitehouse had thrown out a fine shot from Horrobin the ball was returned on the left, and Copeland scored within a couple of minutes of the start, this success being loudly cheered. The Villa got a foul in a good position, but nothing came of it, and though they pressed strongly on the right the visiting defence was sound. Devey broke away and passed to Athersmith, who shot at long range, the ball going just wide of the posts. One of the Walsall men was hurt in a charge from Campbell, the latter being cautioned, but the game was resumed after a short delay. The Villa were soon up by pretty passing, but Athersmith's shot was feeble, and easily cleared by the goalkeeper. Walsall then ran down the left, but the ball was only driven out. Campbell made a pretty run, but shot badly. John Cowan forced a corner, and directly afterwards Bunyan made a capital save from Campbell. The Villa, however, were playing in the tamest fashion, whilst Walsall were straining every nerve, the latter certainly having the best of matters. The visitors effectively packed their goal from a foul close in, whilst Campbell was charged over just as he was shooting. A corner to the Villa was headed over, and then the Walsall goal had a couple of the narrowest escapes. Evans from a foul landed the ball into the net without its having touched anyone, and nothing more was done up to half-time, when Walsall led by a goal to nothing.

On resuming, Walsall were the first to attack, Griffin from a nice centre by Horrobin heading just over the bar. Then the Villa got down, and Devey tried Bunyan with a good one, which the latter threw out. John Cowan forced a corner, but the backs got the ball away, and Spencer headed outside. Campbell skimmed the bar, but Walsall broke away, and whilst Whitehouse was hurt and lay on the ground, J. Aston ran up and scored. Whitehouse's leg was so badly hurt that he had to leave the field. Evans went into goal, Crabtree playing back. John Cowan forced a corner, but the ball was headed outside, and Crabtree landed the ball on top of the net. Whitehouse came out again very lame amidst cheers, but the Villa could make little headway, the bustle and dash of the visitors neutralising all their efforts at pretty, short passing on the wet ground. At length, however, some long crosses ended in Campbell scoring ten minutes from the finish. A foul followed at close quarters, but the ball was got away. Playing in earnest now, the Villa attacked strongly, but Bunyan brought off a fine save from Devey, and though the home side had much the best of it to the finish, there was no more scoring, Walsall winning by 2 goals to 1.

Walsall: Bunyan; Pears and C. L. Aston; Holmes, Wilkes and Taggart; Horrobin, J. Aston, Griffin, Copeland and G. Johnson.

Aston Villa: Whitehouse; Spencer and Evans; Reynolds, James Cowan and Crabtree; Athersmith, Devey, Campbell, Wheldon and John Cowan.

The Double-Winners medal presented to club officials and players.

1st September 1896

Blackburn Rovers v W. B. Albion	1-2
Sheffield W. v Liverpool	1-2
Sunderland v Bury	0-1
Wolverhampton W. v Derby County	1-0

2nd September 1896

Aston Villa v Stoke	**2-1**

5th September 1896

Blackburn Rovers v Liverpool	1-0
Bury v Preston North End	0-0
Derby County v Nottingham Forest	1-1
Everton v Sheffield W.	2-1
Sheffield United v Burnley	1-0
Stoke v Wolverhampton W.	2-1
Sunderland v Bolton Wanderers	1-1
W. B. Albion v Aston Villa	**3-1**

7th September 1896

Burnley v Sunderland	1-1
Liverpool v Bolton Wanderers	0-2

12th September 1896

Aston Villa v Sheffield United	**2-2**
Bolton Wanderers v Blackburn Rovers	0-0
Burnley v Bury	1-0
Liverpool v Derby County	2-0
Nottingham Forest v Stoke	4-0
Preston North End v Sunderland	5-3
Sheffield W. v W. B. Albion	3-1
Wolverhampton W. v Everton	0-1

19th September 1896

Blackburn Rovers v Sheffield W.	4-0
Burnley v Nottingham Forest	2-2
Bury v Liverpool	1-2
Derby County v Wolverhampton W.	4-3
Everton v Aston Villa	**2-3**
Sheffield United v Sunderland	3-0
Stoke v Bolton Wanderers	2-3
W. B. Albion v Preston North End	1-1

26th September 1896

Aston Villa v Everton	**1-2**
Bolton Wanderers v Sunderland	1-0
Derby County v Bury	7-2
Liverpool v W. B. Albion	0-0
Nottingham Forest v Sheffield United	2-2
Preston North End v Burnley	5-3
Sheffield W. v Stoke	4-3
Wolverhampton W. v Blackburn Rovers	1-1

3rd October 1896

Blackburn Rovers v Burnley	3-2
Bolton Wanderers v Preston North End	3-1
Everton v Liverpool	2-1
Sheffield United v Aston Villa	**0-0**
Sunderland v Wolverhampton W.	0-3
W. B. Albion v Sheffield W.	0-2

10th October 1896

Aston Villa v W. B. Albion	**2-0**
Bolton Wanderers v Bury	2-0
Burnley v Everton	2-1
Derby County v Sheffield United	1-3
Liverpool v Nottingham Forest	3-0
Preston North End v Blackburn Rovers	3-1
Sheffield W. v Sunderland	0-0
Wolverhampton W. v Stoke	1-2

17th October 1896

Blackburn Rovers v Bolton Wanderers	1-0
Burnley v Preston North End	2-2
Bury v Sheffield W.	1-1
Derby County v Aston Villa	**1-3**
Everton v Sheffield United	1-2
Stoke v Nottingham Forest	3-0
Sunderland v Liverpool	4-3
W. B. Albion v Wolverhampton W.	1-0

19th October 1896

Sheffield United v Liverpool	1-1

24th October 1896

Aston Villa v Derby County	**2-1**
Bolton Wanderers v Stoke	4-0
Liverpool v Blackburn Rovers	4-0
Nottingham Forest v Burnley	4-1
Preston North End v Sheffield United	1-0
Sheffield W. v Everton	4-1
W. B. Albion v Bury	0-0
Wolverhampton W. v Sunderland	0-1

31st October 1896

Blackburn Rovers v Preston North End	0-4
Bury v Bolton Wanderers	2-2
Everton v Wolverhampton W.	0-0
Nottingham Forest v Sheffield W.	2-2
Sheffield United v Derby County	2-2
Stoke v Aston Villa	**0-2**
W. B. Albion v Liverpool	0-1

2nd November 1896

W. B. Albion v Bolton Wanderers	1-0

7th November 1896

Aston Villa v Bury	**1-1**
Burnley v Blackburn Rovers	0-1
Derby County v Stoke	5-1
Liverpool v Sunderland	3-0
Preston North End v Nottingham F.	3-2

9th November 1896

Stoke v Preston North End	2-1

14th November 1896

Blackburn Rovers v Nottingham Forest	0-0
Bury v Stoke	4-2
Derby County v Burnley	3-2
Everton v Bolton Wanderers	2-3
Preston North End v Liverpool	1-1
Sheffield W. v Aston Villa	**1-3**
W. B. Albion v Sheffield United	0-1

18th November 1896

Nottingham Forest v Derby County	1-2

21st November 1896

Aston Villa v Sheffield W.	**4-0**
Derby County v Blackburn Rovers	6-0
Liverpool v Everton	0-0
Nottingham Forest v Sunderland	2-1
Preston North End v Bolton Wanderers	2-3
Sheffield United v Bury	2-2
Stoke v W. B. Albion	2-2
Wolverhampton W. v Burnley	2-0

28th November 1896

Blackburn Rovers v Aston Villa	**1-5**
Bury v Wolverhampton W.	3-2
Everton v Burnley	6-0
Nottingham Forest v Liverpool	2-0
Preston North End v Stoke	3-0
Sheffield W. v Derby County	2-0
W. B. Albion v Sunderland	1-0

5th December 1896

Sheffield United v W. B. Albion	0-1
Stoke v Derby County	2-2
Sunderland v Sheffield W.	0-0
Wolverhampton W. v Nottingham F.	4-1

7th December 1896

Bolton Wanderers v Everton	2-0

12th December 1896

Liverpool v Bury	3-1
Nottingham Forest v Blackburn Rovers	2-1
Sheffield W. v Wolverhampton W.	0-0
Sunderland v Everton	1-1
W. B. Albion v Stoke	1-2

19th December 1896

Aston Villa v Nottingham Forest	**3-2**
Bolton Wanderers v W. B. Albion	2-2
Burnley v Sheffield W.	1-1
Derby County v Liverpool	3-2
Everton v Stoke	4-2
Sunderland v Blackburn Rovers	0-1
Wolverhampton W. v Preston N. E.	1-1

JAMES WHITEHOUSE

● Stayed with Villa for one more season, sharing the goalkeeping position with Wilkes and new signing Billy George. Moved to Bedminster in May 1898 and returned to Grimsby Town a year later. Also played for Newton Heath, Manchester City, Third Lanark, Hull City and Southend United.

HOWARD SPENCER

● Won another League Championship medal in 1900 and captained Villa to the 1905 FA Cup win. After retiring in 1907, joined the Villa Board in 1909 until ill-health forced his retirement in 1936. Was a successful businessman and died after a long illness in Four Oaks, Sutton Coldfield, January 1940.

ALBERT EVANS

● Despite breaking his leg three times with Villa (and five times in all), Evans won two more League Championship medals with Villa, but missed the 1905 FA Cup win. Left Villa in 1907 for West Bromwich Albion, becoming their trainer two years later. In 1920 he took over as manager of Coventry City, but resigned in 1924 to travel the world, working as a gold prospector in the Yukon and a sheep farmer in Canada. Died in March 1966, aged 92, and was the last surviving member of the 'double' team.

JOHN REYNOLDS

● Was part of a mini-exodus from Villa to Celtic at the end of the 'double' season, but only played a handful of games in Scotland before moving on to Southampton. He died in 1917 at the age of 48.

JAMES COWAN

● Was part of the Villa League Championship sides of 1899 and 1900 before retiring in 1902. Coached the Villa youngsters and ran a local pub. Became Queens Park Rangers first manager in 1906, a position he held until 1913. Died in a London hospital in December 1918, aged 50.

JAMES CRABTREE

● Stayed with Villa until 1902, adding two more League Championship medals (1899 and 1900) before moving to Plymouth Argyle for a season. Returned to Birmingham as a licensee, but died at the age of 36 in June 1908 after a domestic accident in which he was severely scalded.

CHARLES ATHERSMITH

● After two more League Championships, joined Small Heath in the summer of 1901 and played over 100 games for the Blues. Later moved into the licensed trade and was also trainer to Grimsby Town for a couple of seasons. Died suddenly at the home of his mother in Oakengates, Shropshire, in September 1910 at the age of 38; it was thought as a result of an injury to his stomach from his playing days.

JOHN DEVEY

● Captained Villa to another two League Championships (1899 and 1900) and played his last game in the Birmingham League in April 1902. The same year he became a Villa Director and remained on the Board until 1934. Became a successful businessman, running a sports outfitters at Six Ways, Aston for many years. Died in a nursing home in Moseley, Birmingham, in October 1940, aged 73.

25th December 1896		
Blackburn Rovers v Sunderland	1-2	
Bury v Nottingham Forest	2-0	
Derby County v W. B. Albion	8-1	
Liverpool v Aston Villa	**3-3**	

25th December 1896
Blackburn Rovers v Sunderland — 1-2
Bury v Nottingham Forest — 2-0
Derby County v W. B. Albion — 8-1
Liverpool v Aston Villa — **3-3**

26th December 1896
Burnley v Liverpool — 4-1
Derby County v Bolton Wanderers — 1-0
Everton v Sunderland — 5-2
Preston North End v Bury — 2-2
Sheffield United v Sheffield W. — 2-0
W. B. Albion v Blackburn Rovers — 1-0
Wolverhampton W. v Aston Villa — **1-2**

28th December 1896
Nottingham Forest v Bury — 3-0
Sheffield W. v Blackburn Rovers — 6-0
Wolverhampton W. v W. B. Albion — 6-1

29th December 1896
Sheffield United v Bolton Wanderers — 1-0

1st January 1897
Bolton Wanderers v Liverpool — 1-4
Bury v Burnley — 1-1
Sheffield United v Everton — 1-2
Sunderland v Preston North End — 1-1

2nd January 1897
Aston Villa v Burnley — **0-3**
Blackburn Rovers v Wolverhampton W. — 2-0
Liverpool v Sheffield United — 0-0
Nottingham Forest v W. B. Albion — 0-1
Sheffield W. v Preston North End — 1-0
Stoke v Everton — 2-3
Sunderland v Derby County — 1-2

9th January 1897
Burnley v Stoke — 1-3
Derby County v Sheffield W. — 2-1
Everton v Nottingham Forest — 3-1
Sheffield United v Blackburn Rovers — 7-0
Sunderland v Aston Villa — **4-2**
Wolverhampton W. v Liverpool — 1-2

16th January 1897
Aston Villa v Sunderland — **2-1**
Blackburn Rovers v Derby County — 5-2
Burnley v Sheffield United — 1-1
Liverpool v Stoke — 1-0
Nottingham Forest v Bolton Wanderers — 2-0
Preston N. E. v Wolverhampton W. — 4-0
W. B. Albion v Everton — 1-4

23rd January 1897
Derby County v Sunderland — 1-0
Sheffield United v Wolverhampton W. — 1-3
Stoke v Sheffield W. — 0-0
W. B. Albion v Nottingham Forest — 4-0

6th February 1897
Blackburn Rovers v Sheffield United — 1-3
Burnley v Bolton Wanderers — 0-2
Bury v Aston Villa — **0-2**
Everton v Preston North End — 3-4
Stoke v Liverpool — 6-1
W. B. Albion v Derby County — 1-4

8th February 1897
Burnley v Aston Villa — **3-4**

20th February 1897
Blackburn Rovers v Bury — 1-2
Preston North End v Sheffield W. — 2-2
Sheffield United v Nottingham Forest — 0-3
Sunderland v Stoke — 4-1

22nd February 1897
Aston Villa v Preston North End — **3-1**

27th February 1897
Sheffield W. v Bolton Wanderers — 0-0
Stoke v Burnley — 3-2
Sunderland v Sheffield United — 0-1
Wolverhampton W. v Bury — 1-1

2nd March 1897
Bury v Everton — 3-1
Sheffield W. v Sheffield United — 1-1
Sunderland v Burnley — 1-1

4th March 1897
Liverpool v Wolverhampton W. — 3-0

6th March 1897
Blackburn Rovers v Everton — 4-2
Bolton Wanderers v Derby County — 1-3
Nottingham Forest v Aston Villa — **2-4**
Sheffield W. v Burnley — 1-0
Sunderland v W. B. Albion — 2-1
Wolverhampton W. v Sheffield United — 1-1

10th March 1897
Nottingham Forest v Everton — 3-0

13th March 1897
Aston Villa v Liverpool — **0-0**
Bolton Wanderers v Burnley — 2-1
Bury v W. B. Albion — 3-0
Everton v Blackburn Rovers — 0-3
Sheffield United v Preston North End — 0-2
Sunderland v Nottingham Forest — 2-2
Wolverhampton W. v Sheffield W. — 2-0

20th March 1897
Blackburn Rovers v Stoke — 2-1
Bolton Wanderers v Nottingham Forest — 0-0
Burnley v Wolverhampton W. — 0-3
Bury v Sheffield United — 0-1

22nd March 1897
Aston Villa v Bolton Wanderers — **6-2**

27th March 1897
Bolton Wanderers v Aston Villa — 1-2
Bury v Blackburn Rovers — 3-0
Derby County v Preston North End — 2-2
Liverpool v Burnley — 1-2
Sheffield United v Stoke — 1-0

3rd April 1897
Liverpool v Sheffield W. — 2-2
Preston North End v Everton — 4-1
Stoke v Sunderland — 0-1
W. B. Albion v Burnley — 3-0

5th April 1897
Bolton Wanderers v Wolverhampton W. — 1-2
Burnley v Derby County — 2-3
Sheffield W. v Nottingham Forest — 3-0

8th April 1897
Nottingham Forest v Preston N. E. — 0-0

10th April 1897
Bolton Wanderers v Sheffield W. — 2-1
Burnley v W. B. Albion — 5-0
Bury v Derby County — 1-0
Liverpool v Preston North End — 0-0
Nottingham F. v Wolverhampton W. — 1-2
Stoke v Blackburn Rovers — 1-0

12th April 1897
Stoke v Bury — 3-0

15th April 1897
Stoke v Sheffield United — 2-0

16th April 1897
Bolton Wanderers v Sheffield United — 0-2
Bury v Sunderland — 1-1
Everton v Derby County — 5-2
Preston North End v W. B. Albion — 0-0

17th April 1897
Aston Villa v Blackburn Rovers — **3-0**
Everton v W. B. Albion — 6-3
Sheffield W. v Bury — 2-0

19th April 1897
Aston Villa v Wolverhampton W. — **5-0**
Preston North End v Derby County — 0-2

20th April 1897
Derby County v Everton — 0-1
Wolverhampton W. v Bolton W. — 4-0

24th April 1897
Everton v Bury — 1-2

26th April 1897
Preston North End v Aston Villa — **0-1**

JOHN CAMPBELL
● After just two seasons with Villa returned to Celtic and helped them to a Scottish League Championship and two Scottish Cup wins in three years. Moved to Third Lanark in 1903 and added another Scottish League Championship medal to his collection. Died in December 1947.

FRED WHELDON
● Assisted Villa to two more League Championships (1899 and 1900) before moving to West Bromwich Albion in the 1900 close-season. Was a Worcestershire county cricketer and later a publican in Worcester where he died in January 1924.

JOHN COWAN
● Remained at Villa until 1899 when he returned to Scotland. Died at Stranraer in May 1937.

THOMAS WILKES
● Despite occasional appearances was unable to regain a regular place in the side and after a spell on loan joined Stoke in 1899.

JAMES WELFORD
● Transferred to Celtic with Campbell and Reynolds at the end of the 'double' season and won a Scottish League Championship medal in his first season and a Scottish Cup medal the following year. Later moved to Belfast Celtic and helped them to win the Irish League, becoming the first footballer to win English, Scottish and Irish League Championship medals. Died in Glasgow in January 1945 at the age of 75.

JEREMIAH GRIFFITHS
● With very limited opportunities at Villa moved to Bilston Town early in the 1897-98 season.

FRED BURTON
● Unable to gain a regular place in the side and retired at the end of the 1897-98 season.

ROBERT CHATT
● After one more season with Villa returned to his native North-East in June 1898, joining Stockton. Reverted to amateur status and won an Amateur FA Cup winners medal in 1899.

STEPHEN SMITH
● Added League Championship medals in 1899 and 1900 with Villa before moving to Portsmouth in October 1901. Helped Pompey to win the Southern League in 1902 and became player-manager of New Brompton four years later. Died in Oxford, May 1935.

VILLA LEAGUE AND CUP CAREERS

	Apps		Goals	
	L	C	L	C
Charlie Athersmith	270	38	75	10
Fred Burton	52	1	2	1
John Campbell	55	8	39	4
Bob Chatt	87	9	19	7
James Cowan	316	38	21	5
John Cowan	64	5	25	2
James Crabtree	178	22	6	1
John Devey	268	38	169	18
Albert Evans	179	24	0	0
Jeremiah Griffiths	2	1	0	0
John Reynolds	96	14	17	0
Steve Smith	169	22	35	7
Howard Spencer	259	35	2	0
Jimmy Welford	79	4	1	0
Fred Wheldon	124	14	68	6
James Whitehouse	40	3	0	0
Tommy Wilkes	44	11	0	0

ASTON VILLA FC INCOME ACCOUNT

from 30th April, 1896, to 30th April, 1897.

Dr.	£	s	d	£	s	d
To Wages, Transfers, and Commission paid to and for players ...				3,999	10	7
To Players' Bonuses for Wins				621	7	6
To Match Expenses viz.:						
Travelling, Training, and other expenses	1,215	4	11			
Footballs, Jerseys, Boots, and Sundries	79	18	3			
Trainer's Wages and Expenses	153	19	4			
Gatekeepers and Groundmen	218	2	4			
Police	78	13	0			
Referees and Linesmen	80	4	11			
Doctors Fees, &c.	44	4	6			
				1,870	7	3
To Gate Money paid away				1,659	9	9
To Printing and Advertising, viz.:						
Stationery, Posters, Tickets, &c.	98	2	0			
Posting and Advertising	121	5	10			
				219	7	10
To General Expenses, viz.:						
Rent, Rates, and Taxes of Ground	472	15	11			
Ground Maintenance and Improvements, &c.	65	2	$0\frac{1}{2}$			
Postages and Telegrams	41	18	$6\frac{1}{2}$			
Association and League Fees	10	0	6			
Petty Payments and Sundries	83	4	9			
Medals for Players	5	16	6			
Club House and Office Rent, Rates,						
Taxes, Insurance, Gas, Coal, Caretakers, &c.	148	8	5			
Secretary's and Assistant's Salaries	258	11	8			
Donations	35	14	6			
Law Accountants' and Bankers' Charges	61	18	8			
				1,183	11	6
To Amount written off Fixtures, Fittings &c.				53	0	0
To Interest on Debentures				80	0	0
To Balance being Profit for the 12 months				1,299	7	$8\frac{1}{2}$
				£10,986	2	$1\frac{1}{2}$

Cr.	£	s	d			
By Members' Subscriptions	268	16	6			
By Season Tickets	191	2	0			
By Gate Money	10,001	8	7			
By Rents	349	5	3			
By Interest on Birmingham Corporation Stock	7	14	8			
By Profit on Sale of Birmingham Corporation Stock	45	12	$1\frac{1}{2}$			
By Accidental Insurance Compensation (less Premiums paid)	82	0	0			
By Sundry Receipts	40	3	0			
	£10,986	2	$1\frac{1}{2}$			

Sep 1	F	h	Small Heath	W	3-1	Wheldon 2, Crabtree	3,000
2	FL	h	Stoke	W	2-1	John Cowan, Devey	6,000
5	FL	a	West Bromwich Albion	L	1-3	Devey	10,000
10	F	a	Grimsby Town	D	3-3	Wheldon 2, Welford	4,000
12	FL	h	Sheffield United	D	2-2	Wheldon, Burton	5,000
19	FL	a	Everton	W	3-2	Campbell 2, Devey	20,000
21	F	a	Leicester Fosse	W	3-2	Smith, Campbell, Devey	2,000
26	FL	h	Everton	L	1-2	Devey	20,000
Oct 3	FL	a	Sheffield United	D	0-0		10,000
5	F	h	Derby County	W	2-1	Devey, Wheldon	2,000
10	FL	h	West Bromwich Albion	W	2-0	Wheldon, Campbell	15,500
17	FL	a	Derby County	W	3-1	John Cowan, Campbell, Wheldon	8,500
19	SC	a	West Bromwich Albion	L	1-2	Wheldon	5,000
24	FL	h	Derby County	W	2-1	Wheldon, John Cowan	7,500
31	FL	a	Stoke	W	2-0	Wheldon, Smith	6,000
Nov 7	FL	h	Bury	D	1-1	Athersmith	5,000
14	FL	a	Sheffield Wednesday	W	3-1	Wheldon, Campbell, Athersmith	8,000
21	FL	h	Sheffield Wednesday	W	4-0	Smith, Devey, Wheldon, Athersmith	14,000
28	FL	a	Blackburn Rovers	W	5-1	Devey, Smith, Wheldon 3	7,000
30	F	a	Stoke	L	0-3		2,000
Dec 5	F	a	Corinthians	D	4-4	Wheldon 2, Devey, Campbell	4,500
7	F	a	Woolwich Arsenal	W	3-1	Wheldon, Cowan, Devey	6,000
12	FL	a	Burnley *(Abandoned)*	–	2-1	Athersmith, Crabtree	
14	BC1	a	Berwick Rangers	W	5-1	Devey 2, Smith, Wheldon, Crabtree	1,500
19	FL	h	Nottingham Forest	W	3-2	Devey, Athersmith, Reynolds	7,000
25	FL	a	Liverpool	D	3-3	James Cowan, Wheldon, Athersmith	15,000
26	FL	a	Wolverhampton W.	W	2-1	Chatt, Athersmith	18,000
29	F	h	Small Heath	D	1-1	Smith	3,500
Jan 2	FL	h	Burnley	L	0-3		14,000
9	FL	a	Sunderland	L	2-4	Ferguson (og), Campbell	8,000
11	F	a	Small Heath	L	1-2	Griffiths	1,500
16	FL	h	Sunderland	W	2-1	Devey, Wheldon	15,000
23	F	a	Tottenham	D	2-2	Athersmith, Devey	3,000
25	BC2	a	West Bromwich Albion	L	1-2	Campbell	4,500
30	EC1	h	Newcastle United	W	5-0	Wheldon 3, Athersmith, Smith	6,000
Feb 6	FL	a	Bury	W	2-0	Campbell 2	10,000
8	FL	a	Burnley	W	4-3	Devey 3, Campbell	4,000
13	EC2	h	Notts County	W	2-1	Wheldon, Campbell	4,000
22	FL	h	Preston North End	W	3-1	Devey 2, Athersmith	14,000
27	EC3	a	Preston North End	D	1-1	Campbell	14,000
Mar 3	EC3R	h	Preston North End	D	0-0		12,000
6	FL	a	Nottingham Forest	W	4-2	Devey 2, Wheldon, John Cowan	8,000
10	EC3R	n*	Preston North End	W	3-2	Athersmith 2, Campbell	22,000
13	FL	h	Liverpool	D	0-0		18,000
20	ECSF	n*	Liverpool	W	3-0	John Cowan 2, Athersmith	30,000
22	FL	h	Bolton Wanderers	W	6-2	Athersmith, Reynolds, Devey, Campbell, Wheldon 2	8,000
27	FL	a	Bolton Wanderers	W	2-1	Wheldon 2	7,000
Apr 3	F	a	Bristol & District	W	4-0	Wheldon, Harvey, Burton, Smith	4,000
10	ECF	n†	Everton	W	3-2	Campbell, Wheldon, Crabtree	65,891
17	FL	h	Blackburn Rovers	W	3-0	Campbell, John Cowan, Kelean (og)	15,000
19	FL	h	Wolverhampton W.	W	5-0	John Cowan 2, Devey, Campbell 2	35,000
24	MC	h	Walsall	D	1-1	Wheldon	8,000
26	FL	a	Preston North End	W	1-0	Wheldon	3,000
28	F	h	West Bromwich Albion	W	3-1	Devey 3	1,000
29	F	a	Notts County	W	2-1	*(Goalscorers not recorded)*	3,000
30	MCR	h	Walsall	L	1-2	Campbell	1,000

(F) Friendly/Testimonial, (FL) Football League, (EC) English Cup, (BC) Birmingham Senior Cup (SC) Staffordshire Cup (MC) Mayor's Cup
* Played at Bramall Lane, Sheffield. † Played at the Crystal Palace.

Jottings at the Aston Villa v. Everton.

CRABTREE TACKLING.

AN ANXIOUS MOMENT. A FREE KICK NEAR THE EVERTON GOAL.

BRIGGS SAVED WELL & WAS KEPT BUSY

ATHERSMITH GETTING AWAY.

A FOUL AGAINST EVERTON MOST INDIGNANT. J. WALSHE 96.

WHITEHOUSE ON THE DEFENCE.

FINAL TABLE • LEAGUE DIVISION ONE 1896/97												
	P	W	D	L	F	A	W	D	L	F	A	Pts
Aston Villa	30	10	3	2	36	16	11	2	2	37	22	47
Sheffield United	30	6	4	5	22	16	7	6	2	20	13	36
Derby County	30	10	2	3	45	22	6	2	7	25	28	36
Preston North End	30	8	4	3	35	21	3	8	4	20	19	34
Liverpool	30	7	6	2	25	10	5	3	7	21	28	33
Sheffield Wednesday	30	9	4	2	29	11	1	7	7	13	26	31
Everton	30	8	1	6	42	29	6	2	7	20	28	31
Bolton Wanderers	30	7	3	5	22	18	5	3	7	18	25	30
Bury	30	7	5	3	25	15	3	5	7	14	29	30
Wolverhampton W.	30	6	4	5	26	14	5	2	8	19	27	28
Nottingham Forest	30	8	3	4	30	16	1	5	9	14	33	26
West Bromwich Alb.	30	7	2	6	18	16	3	4	8	15	40	26
Stoke	30	8	3	4	30	18	3	0	12	18	41	25
Blackburn Rovers	30	8	1	6	27	25	3	2	10	8	37	25
Sunderland	30	4	6	5	21	21	3	3	9	13	26	23
Burnley	30	4	5	6	25	25	2	2	11	18	36	19